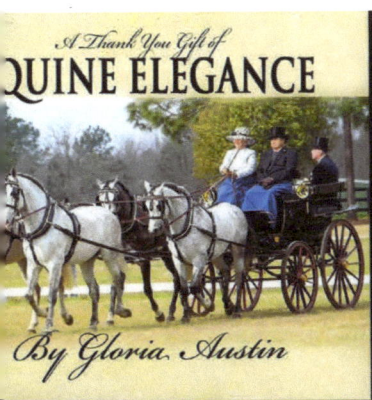

More New Titles Coming Soon

Why Not Own EHI's Entire Library of Equine Knowledge?
https://amzn.to/2NsUoeX

EQUINE HERITAGE INSTITUTE

More New Titles Coming Soon

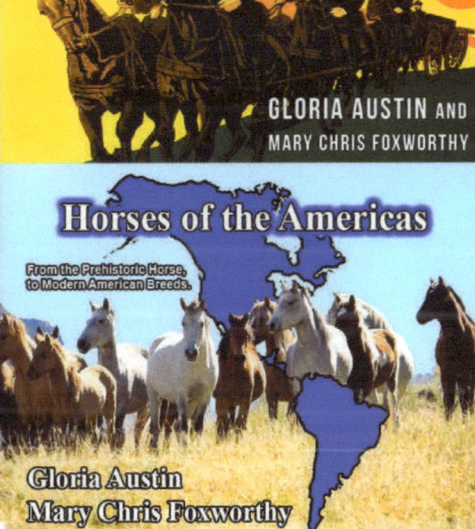
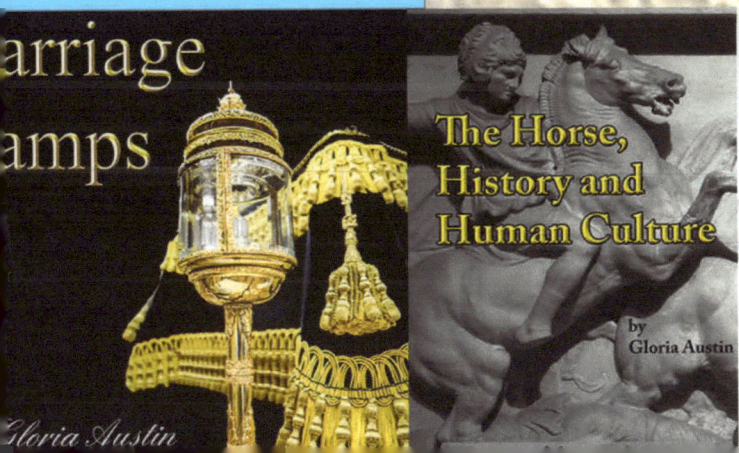

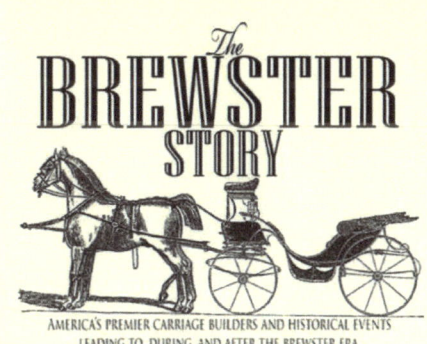

Our Mission: To educate, Celebrate, and preserve the history of the horse and its role in shaping World Civilization and changing lives.

http://www.equineheritageinstitute.org
http://www.equineheritagemuseum.com

EQUINE HERITAGE INSTITUTE

For information, please contact: Gloria Austin
3024 Marion County Road
Weirsdale, Fl. 32195
Phone: (352)753-2826

Horses of North America
From the Prehistoric Horse, To Feral Horses, To
Modern American Breeds.
The History of Horses in America.
By: Gloria Austin and Mary Chris Foxworthy
President of: Equine Heritage Institute, Inc. (EHI)

First Publish Date 2018
Copyright © 2018 by Equine Heritage Institute, Inc.

All rights reserved. No part of this publication may be reproduced, distributed, or transmitted in any form or by any means, including photocopying, recording, or other electronic or mechanical methods, without the prior written permission of the publisher, except in the case of brief quotations embodied in critical reviews and certain other noncommercial uses permitted by copyright law. For permission requests, write to the publisher, addressed "Attention: Permissions Coordinator," at the address below.

Gloria Austin Carriage Collection, LLC; Equine Heritage Institute, Inc.
3024 Marion County Road Weirsdale, FL 32195 Office: (352) 753-2826 Fax: (352) 753-6186

Ordering Information:
Quantity sales: Special discounts are available on quantity purchases by corporations, associations, and others. For details, contact the publisher at the address above.
Printed in the United States of America
First Edition ISBN 978-1-7320805-6-0

TABLE OF CONTENTS

ORIGINS OF HORSES IN THE AMERICAS 6

THE DAWN HORSE 8

MEANWHILE ACROSS THE ATLANTIC 11

HORSES RETURN TO AMERICA 22

BRING ON THE BREEDS! 51

TYPES OF HORSES THAT CAME TO THE AMERICAS 52

THE PURPOSE OF HORSES IN THE EARLY AMERICAS 60

IN THE BEGINNING……BREEDING FOR THE PURPOSE 65

BREEDS OF THE AMERICAS 67

MODERN BREEDS AND USAGE 113

CONCLUSION 116

SOURCES 117

ORIGINS OF HORSES IN THE AMERICAS

Forward

Most people think of history and civilization as being made and created by men, but often, history and the development of human societies and civilizations are drastically altered by the introduction of an influential catalyst. Some of those influential catalysts from our past are fire, the wheel, metal, agriculture, religion, and written language but one is missing in the typical history books, and it comes in the form of an animal. The horse transformed the world once its speed and power were harnessed. It is the first thing that allowed a man to travel faster than his two legs could carry him on land.

Some people talk about the Stone, Copper, Bronze, and Iron Ages while others talk about the Ancient World, Middle Ages, Age of Discovery, Revolution and Industry, and The Modern World. A student of the social history of the horse might look at things differently. The Horse Eras might look like this:

Era of Consumption (50,000BC to present)

Era of Utilization and Status (4000BC to 1900AD)

Era of Herding (3500BC to present)

Era of the Chariot (1700BC-400AD)

Era of the Cavalry (700BC – 1942AD)

Era of Agriculture (900AD – 1945AD)

Era of the Carriage (1700AD-1920AD)

Era of Leisure – (1900 to present)

Throughout history, the horse was used for food, herding, warfare, transportation, communication, agriculture, trade, commerce, pleasure, sport, and competition. This is to say nothing about its significant role in the transfer of language, culture, and technology that resulted with the increased mobility the horse offered to man. The horse and wheel gave a great boost to man's ability to move goods from place to place. A man can carry about 50 pounds, a horse can pack 200 pounds, but a horse and a wheeled vehicle can transport up to twice the horses own weight; consequently, a 1,000-pound horse could move 2,000 pounds of cargo. The horse has had an impact on the world – everywhere it went and on every aspect of life.

It is fascinating to look at the history of the horse in the Americas. Most people do not realize that the many horse breeds of the Americas that we are familiar with have developed here in only the last 500 years. 500 years ago, there were 60,000,000 bison, thousands of deer and dogs in North America and llamas in South America. There were no hogs, horses or cattle; these animals had to come from Europe with the early explorers, early settlers and colonists

Archeologists and anthropologists, through the study of a very long and contiguous fossil sequence, suggest that the horse's ancestors originated, lived, and evolved in North America for 55 million years, and eventually migrated around the globe. The horse eventually disappeared in the Americas. Even though the predecessor of our horse lived here in prehistoric times the horse, as we know it today, was brought to the America's by the Spanish, French, and English who started to explore the new world in the 1500s. Over the years, and through the introduction of stock from many European sources, the United States has ended up with a more diverse equine population than any other country in the world. We are a multi-cultural country of many religions and races, and our horse population reflects this same diversity.

The relatively new (27-year-old) field of molecular biology, using mitochondrial-DNA analysis, has recently found that there is some conflicting evidence as to the origin of horse breeds in America; but regardless, the recorded history of horse breeds, as we know them in the Americas now, began in the 1500s.

A study commissioned by the American Horse Council Foundation and conducted by the Barents Group concluded that there are currently 9.2 million horses in the United States alone! That is amazing since there were no horses in the Americas before the 1500s. Horses were brought to the Americas, mostly by Europeans, and now the United States alone has more horses than all of Europe; Europe has a little over 6 million horses.

The evolutionary lineage of the horse is among the best-documented in all paleontology. The history of the horse family, Equidae, began during the Eocene Epoch, which lasted from about 55.8 million to 33.9 million years ago. The dinosaurs are gone. Mammals roam the earth consisting of mostly smaller species, rodents, and birds, though it's also the time when rhinos and elephants emerge.

In 2015 brothers Mark and Mike Oliver were digging fossils near Lake Kemmerer in Wyoming. They were collecting ancient fish fossils hoping to find a nice specimen to sell. Unexpectedly, they unearthed a small talus bone. Fish fossils are common in the area, but a talus bone was unusual. They sought assistance from local experts, and after careful hours of extrication, they found her - Eohippus. They named her "Olive." She drowned in the ancient lake, buried in the fine grain sediment. As the Rocky Mountains began to uplift, and the climate became drier, the lake dried. The mud encasing Olive baked in the sun for millions of years preserving her skeleton until the Oliver brothers found her. Most fossils are found as disparate pieces to be reassembled, Olive was preserved in articulation, fully intact save a small piece of missing pelvis. *(left)* She is one of only a handful of any ancient species found intact. Common and unremarkable during her lifetime, Olive is a treasure today and the find of a lifetime for two archeologist brothers. *(cited from: http://www.horsenation.com/2016/10/04/warhorses-the-dawn-horse/)*

For 20 million years there were few evolutionary changes for little Eohippus. Then, very slowly the Earth began to change. The continents broke and drifted apart. In North America, the mountain ranges began to uplift. In the center of the continents, the climate became drier. Lakes dried; their once-muddy bottoms eventually formed rock. The forests gave way to grassy plains. Seasons became more evident, and ice began to form at the poles. Life reacted to these changes, and Eohippus was gone. *(cited from http://www.horsenation.com/2016/10/04/warhorses-the-dawn-horse/)*

THE EVOLUTION OF THE HORSE.

Age	Epoch	Formations in Western United States and Characteristic Type of Horse in Each	Fore Foot	Hind Foot	Teeth
Quaternary or Age of Man	Recent	Equus	One Toe, Splints of 2nd and 4th digits	One Toe, Splints of 2nd and 4th digits	Long-Crowned, Cement-covered
	Pleistocene				
Tertiary or Age of Mammals	Pliocene	BLANCO, OGALALLA — Pliohippus			
	Miocene	ARIKAREE — Merychippus	Three Toes, Side toes not touching the ground	Three Toes, Side toes not touching the ground	
	Oligocene	JOHN DAY, WHITE RIVER — Mesohippus	Three Toes, Side toes touching the ground; splint of 5th digit	Three Toes, Side toes touching the ground	Short-Crowned, without Cement
	Eocene	UINTA, BRIDGER — Orohippus; WASATCH — Eohippus	Four Toes	Three Toes, Splints of 1st and 5th digits	
	Paleocene	PUERCO AND TORREJON			
Age of Reptiles	Cretaceous, Jurassic, Triassic				

* There is some conflicting evidence whether horses completely disappeared in the Americas until the 1500s but regardless, the recorded history of horse breeds, as we know them in America now, began in the 1500s

Although Eohippus fossils occur in both the Old and the New World, the subsequent evolution of the horse took place chiefly in North America. Modern horses, zebras, and asses belong to the genus Equus, the only surviving genus in a once diverse family, the Equidae. Based on fossil records, the genus appears to have originated in North America about 4 million years ago and spread to Eurasia; presumably by crossing the Bering land bridge 2 to 3 million years ago. Following that original emigration, there were additional westward migrations to Asia and return migrations back to North America, as well as several extinctions of Equus species in North America. The last prehistoric North American horses died out between 13,000 and 11,000 years ago, at the end of the Pleistocene, but by then Equus had spread to Asia, Europe, and Africa. *(cited from https://www.livescience.com/9589-surprising-history-America-wild-horses.html).*

Meanwhile Across the Atlantic

The Pre-Domestic Horse

If we had no evidence from fossils, it would still be apparent from the evidence of European cave paintings alone that, in the Old Stone Age, a great variety of wild horse types roamed Europe. During the upper Paleolithic era- between 40,000 and 10,000 years ago. Prehistoric people in Europe and Asia and elsewhere depicted the animals they saw in thousands of cave art drawings. The greatest concentration of cave art occurs in southern France and northern Spain where horses and bison are the most frequently depicted animals. There are drawings on cave roofs in the Dordogne that depict identically the present day Exmoor ponies. In Les Combarelles caves there are drawings of an obese, ram-headed Clydesdale looking animal. In the Pyrenees, there is a very credible Fell pony drawing. In Font de Gaume caves there are New Forest ponies in the act of leaping.

Domestication of Horses

Horses have played an important role in the history of the world! Whether ridden or driven, horses were the means by which cultures intermingled, people were able to share communications, wars were waged and nations developed. To determine when and where the horse was first domesticated is difficult. The first known written work on horses was "The Chariot Training Manual" by Kikkulis the Mittanite in 1345 BC yet we have irrefutable evidence of the use of horses as early as 5000 BC. In the manual, he gives detailed information about grooming, training, and care of the horse *(left: Horses groomed and watered. From a stone panel from the North-West Palace of Ashurnasirpal (northern Iraq), 883-859 BC)*

In 430 BC a Greek named Xenophon wrote "The Art of Horsemanship." It is the first fully preserved manual on the art of riding horses. He differs from other ancient writers on the horse because he encouraged mutual respect between man and horse. Xenophon's methods were very advanced for the time but he was still at a major disadvantage–he lacked a saddle!

The first saddles constructed around solid trees first appeared during the Han dynasty in the year 200 BC. With the invention of the solid tree along came the invention of the stirrup as we know it today. By 477 AD the stirrup was widespread across China and then spread into Europe. The saddle tree and the stirrup offered great support for the rider. Horses could now be used more effectively in battle. Through the centuries, countries and continents changed their ruling classes and borders many times via warfare on the back of a horse. By the 1500s and 1600s horsemanship was considered an art much the same as music, painting, and literature.

Breeding of Horses

Horse breeding records are some of the most impressive efforts to chronicle animal lineages in human history, with some stretching back thousands of years. Yet decoding the genetic origins of today's horses has proved remarkably difficult. A new study finds that nearly all modern horse breeds can be traced to two distinct, ancient Middle Eastern lines that were brought to Europe about 700 years ago. Researchers have found that two major lineages are responsible for almost all modern horses: Arabian horses from the Arabian Peninsula and the Turkoman horses from the Eurasian Steppe. Some of these horses would have arrived in Europe with merchants, others would have been gifts between rulers, and still, others might have been captured during warfare. Over hundreds of years, European horse breeders found that stallions from these Arabian and Turkoman lines produced more desirable offspring, repeatedly reinforcing those two lineages in their breeding programs until they were practically ubiquitous. Today, they form the patrilineal backbone of nearly every modern horse breed. *(cited from http://www.sciencemag.org/news/2017/06/most-modern-horses-came-just-two-ancient-lineages)*

Now raised in a remote area of Central Asia, dwindling numbers of Turkomans *(left)* continue to exist and are proof of the merit of a strangely lovely horse. They were said to be ewe necked and slab-sided. But the proper Turkoman is in fact, an elegant, tall horse with a conformation to suit his environment and his job. There are several breeds or strains within the Turkoman area in northeastern Iran that includes the Akhal, the Yomud, the Goklan, and Nokhorli. *(cited from http://www.museumofthehorse.org/a-look-at-the-turkoman-horse-in-iran/)*

The Arabian *(right)* is the oldest purebred in the world and foundation horse for many modern light breeds. The first Arabian breeders were the tribesmen of Arabia; Bedouins, who valued the Arabian horse above all other possessions. The Bedouins, very selective in their breeding programs, put the greatest emphasis on performance and allowed only the finest horses to reproduce. Stamina, soundness, speed, disposition, and loyalty were paramount. *(cited from: http://www.scottsdaleshow.com/club-info/breed-information)*

During the early middle ages, horse breeding was a fairly stagnant practice, with the majority of animals not leaving the region of their birth. Interregional trade was slow, and horses were no exception. Breeding programs were then, necessarily, somewhat closed gene pools. Medieval Europe bred large horses specifically for war, called destriers. *(left)* These horses were the ancestors of the great heavy horses of today, and their size was preferred not simply because of the weight of the armor, but also because a large horse provided more power for the knight's lance. Weighing almost twice as much as a normal riding horse, the destrier was a powerful weapon in battle.

On the other hand, during this same time, lighter horses were bred in northern Africa and the Middle East by Muslim warriors, who preferred a faster, more agile horse. *(right)* The lighter horse suited the raids and battles of the Bedouins, allowing them to outmaneuver rather than overpower the enemy. When Muslim warriors and European knights collided in warfare, the heavy knights were frequently outmaneuvered.

The Europeans, however, soon made up for the lack of speed of their native breeds by incorporating genetic traits from captured oriental horses such as the Arabian to their stables. This cross-breeding led both to a nimbler war horse, such as today's Percheron, but also created a type of horse known as a Courser, a predecessor to the Thoroughbred, which was used as a message horse.

Horses generally have three gaits: walk, trot, and canter. Any gait between walk and canter is considered an "intermediate" gait. A horse that performs an intermediate gait other than the trot is today called "gaited," or in medieval terms an "ambler." Thomas Blundeville, in 1565, cautioned breeders of military animals to select strongly trotting mares and mentions that these may be difficult to find inside England. His advice suggests that non-trotting gaits were a fairly widespread trait, but undesirable for martial activity. As battlefield technology continued to evolve, and the sport of jousting became increasingly discouraged, the ménage became the new aristocratic outlet. Ménage is considered the root of the modern sport of dressage and consisted of performing complex equestrian movements. Because of this, gaitedness in the general population was further discouraged. While having a strong trot was useful on the battlefield, it was critical for the ménage.

With the development of new "types" of horses, corresponding to new human social roles came new breeding practices. While before any two quality animals might be matched (with occasional exceptions due to relatedness), now the match was expected to be a similar type of horse. This is perhaps the root of modern breed classifications though again most of these animals are a "type" and not yet considered of a "breed."
(cited from http://www.medievalists.net/2015/12/horse-power-social-evolution-in-medieval-europe/)

(left: horse drawing of Leonardo Da Vinci 1452-1519 - Da Vinci studied both the anatomy and physiology of animals in order to render them with scientific precision)

During the Renaissance, horses were bred not only for war, but for Haute Ecole riding, derived from the most athletic movements required of a warhorse, and popular among the elite nobility of the time. Breeds such as the Lipizzan were developed from Spanish-bred horses for this purpose, and also became the preferred mounts of cavalry officers, who were derived mostly from the ranks of the nobility.

The Pure Spanish Horse (PRE) was unified as a breed in the sixteenth century (between 1567 and 1593) by the Spanish King Felipe II *(left)* who formally established the standards for the breed which we recognize today as the Pure Spanish Horse.

Throughout the Renaissance and Baroque periods, the PRE was well known for his superiority throughout Europe. Riding academies were formed in Austria, France, Italy, Germany and Portugal where dressage and high school movements were developed, refined and flourished. The PRE was the favored mount of the academies for its impulsion, forward motion, and agility.

Horse racing is one of the oldest of all sports, and its basic concept has undergone virtually no change over the centuries.

Charles II established Newmarket as the headquarters of English racing. *(left)*

Racing in medieval England began when horses for sale were ridden in competition by professional riders to display the horses' speed to buyers. During the reign of Richard the Lionheart (1189–99), the first known racing purse was offered, £40, for a race run over a 3-mile (4.8-km) course with knights as riders.

In the 16th century, Henry VIII imported horses from Italy and Spain (presumably Barbs) and established studs at several locations. In the 17th century James I sponsored race meets in England. His successor, Charles I, had a stud of 139 horses when he died in 1649.

Charles II (reigned 1660–85) became known as "the father of the English turf" and inaugurated the King's Plates, races for which prizes were awarded to the winners. His articles for these races were the earliest national racing rules. The horses raced were 6 years old and carried 168 pounds (76 kg), and the winner was the first to win two 4-mile (6.4-km) heats. The patronage of

In France, the first documented horse race was held in 1651 as the result of a wager between two noblemen. During the reign of Louis XIV (1643–1715), racing based on gambling was prevalent. Louis XVI (reigned 1774–93) organized a jockey club and established rules of racing by royal decree that included requiring certificates of origin for horses and imposing extra weight on foreign horses. *(cited from https://www.britannica.com/sports/horse-racing)*

Thus, was the state of "horse breeding" in Europe when explorers started to bring horses to the Americas and it gives us an idea of the types of horses that may have come with the early explorers and settlers. Europeans had the benefit of the horse's speed and strength for thousands of years.

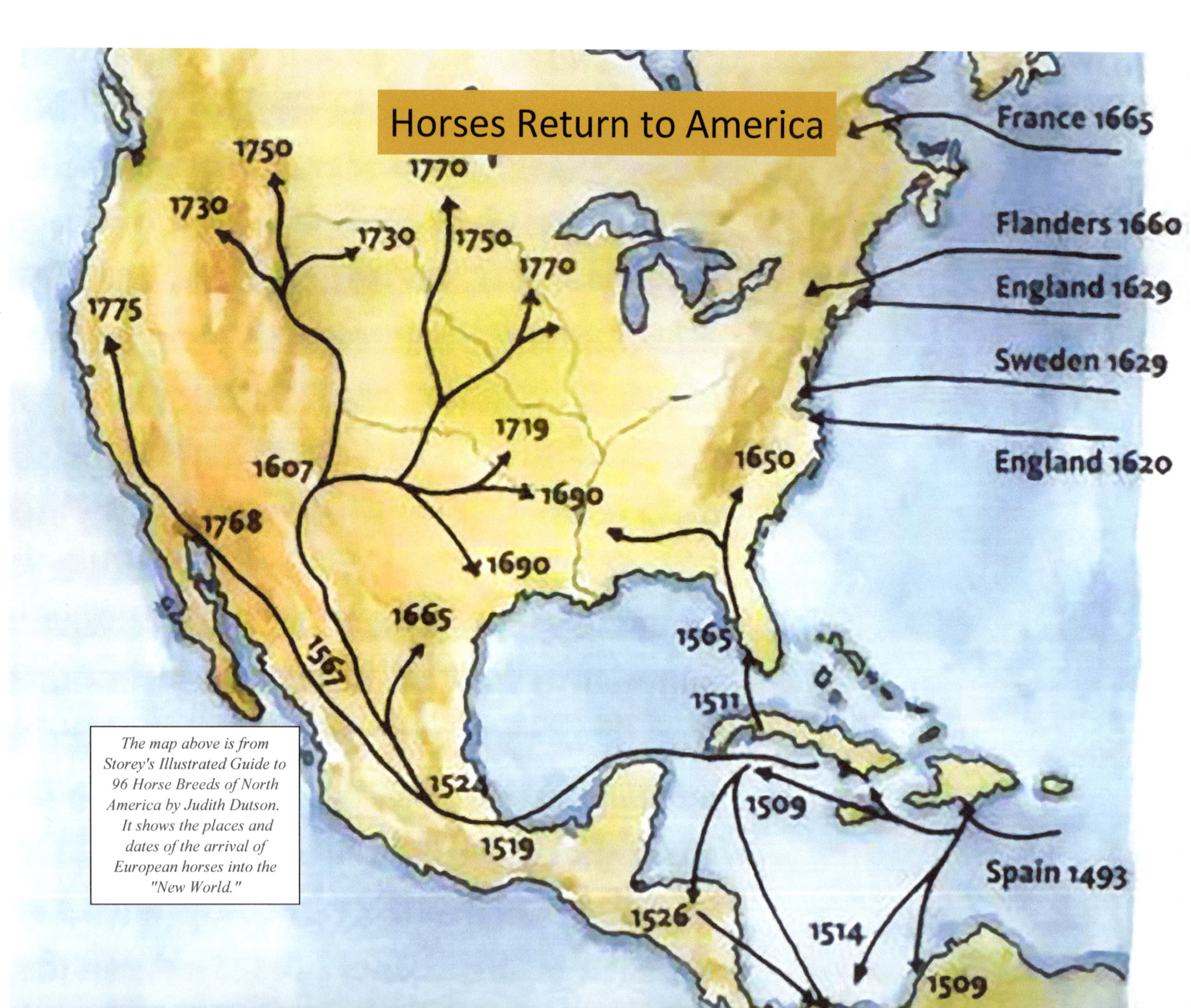

Transportation of Horses

The common method for loading horses on ships in that era was to blindfold then hoist them on board by means of a belly sling and a crane. Once on deck and in their stalls, they were again suspended by belly slings for the voyage with their front feet hobbled and just touching the deck then they were tethered by restraining lines to prevent injury. The standard practice with horses was to suspend the animals in these slings, or "horse hammocks," during calm weather and then lower them completely to the deck in rough seas; otherwise they would be mercilessly tossed about if left suspended.

When a ship anchored off the coast of the New World, the horses that survived the voyage were brought out of their stalls in the ship's hold. In order to prevent the horses from panicking, they were blindfolded and carefully raised from below deck by hoists attached to slings surrounding the horses' bodies. In these early days before wharves were built, the horses were lowered into the water and made to swim ashore, led by men in rowboats.

1493

Christopher Columbus was well received in the court of King Ferdinand and Queen Isabella after his first voyage in 1492. *(left)* The first horses known to arrive in the New World were transported by Christopher Columbus on his second voyage *(below)* in 1493. In a letter of May 23, 1493, to their secretary Fernando de Zafra, Ferdinand and Isabella wrote, "Among the persons which we order to go in the above-mentioned armada we have agreed that twenty lancers are to sail with horses. Five of them shall bring spare horses and those horses shall be mares." This suggests that the breeding of horses in the new colony was a priority.

The lancers were provided with meager funds and were required to be in Seville by June 20 to be ready to set sail.

The lancer's acquired their horses from horse traders from either the plains of the Rio Guadalquivir near Cordova or from the area of salt marshes formed where the Guadalquivir empties into the Atlantic Ocean. There is some inconsistency in accounts, but the most reliable accounts state that 24 stallions and 10 mares were loaded. 25 of these horses belonged to the lancers while the remainder belonged to Columbus. There was some tit-for-tat trading on the part of the underpaid lancers. They had received money from Columbus with directions to purchase all of their horses plus those for the Columbus. The men bought worthy war horses for themselves, but instead of buying quality horses for Columbus they purchased in his words, "regrettable beasts" and pocketed the savings. Columbus complained of their trickery to the King and Queen to no avail.

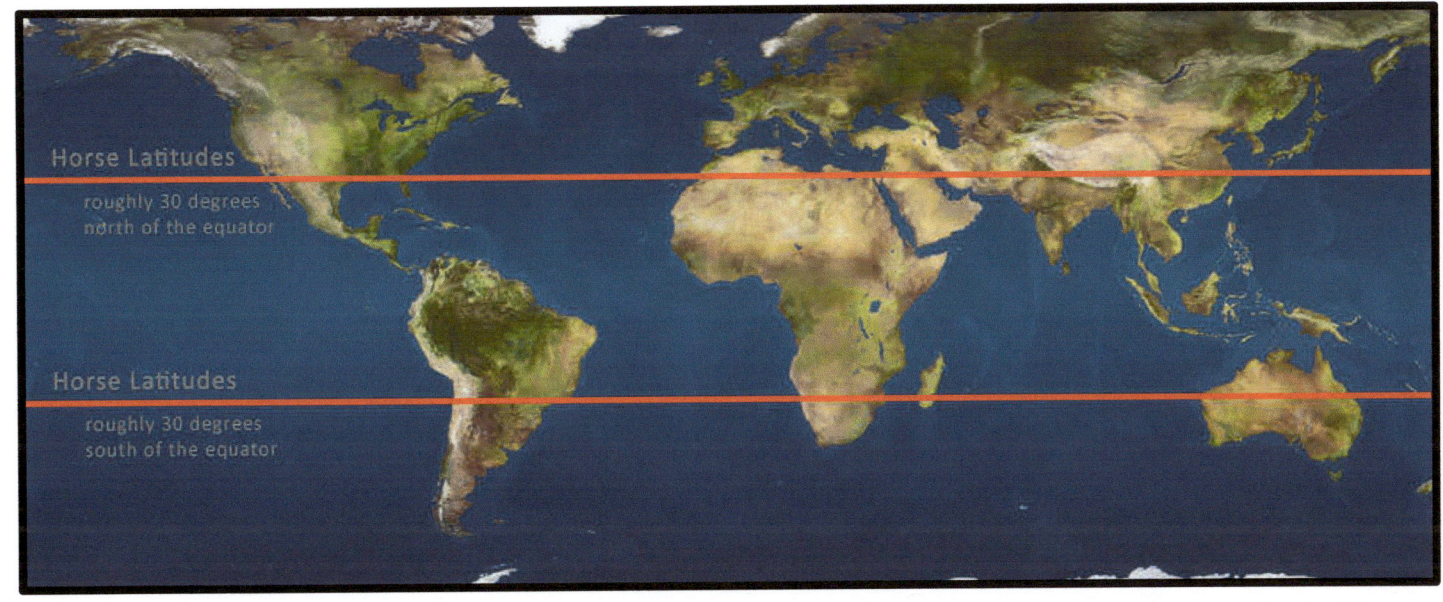

There is no record of how many horses arrived in the New World. In those times the typical mortality rate for livestock aboard sailing ships has been estimated at about one third. The Atlantic Ocean between Spain and Canary Islands was referred to as the "Gulf of Mares" because at times it was littered with floating carcasses of equine shipping fatalities. That section of the Atlantic Ocean is also known as the "Horse Latitudes." *(above)* On November 19, 1493, Christopher Columbus discovered the island of Puerto Rico in his second voyage to the New World. He found the island populated by as many as 50,000 Taíno or Arawak Indians. The Taíno Indians who greeted Columbus made a big mistake when they showed him gold nuggets in the river and told him to take all he wanted. Originally the newcomers called the island San Juan Bautista, for St. John the Baptist and the town was named Puerto Rico ("rich port") for its abundance of natural resources, especially gold. An eyewitness to the unloading, Guglielmo Coma, conveyed the following, "Guacanagari (a friendly local Taino chief) came down to the shore to see the ships. When there, he admired the lofty bulwarks, examined the tackle of the ships, observed attentively the instruments of iron, but fixed his eye most upon the horses of which the Indians were entirely destitute. A great number of fine horses fleet for the course and strong to bear armor – had been brought out by the Spaniards. These horses had plated bits, trappings of gay colors, and straps highly polished. The formidable appearance of these animals was not without terror to the Indians, for they suspected they fed on human flesh."

By 1494 Columbus was so convinced of the value of horses for military and civilian use that he wrote to the Spanish sovereign requesting that horses be included on all future voyages. His request was favorably received, and for several years each fleet's manifest included horses, especially broodmares. Mandatory shipments of horses from Spain ceased about 30 years after their arrival in the New World. *(cited from Wild Horses of the West: History and Politics of American Mustangs, pp 55-59)*

Number of horses brought: 35 - Number of horses survived: unknown

1508

Spanish colonization of Puerto Rico began in 1508. King Ferdinand II of Aragon assigned Ponce de León to lead an official expedition to the island. Agüeybaná was one of the two principal and most powerful leaders of the Taíno people when the Spaniards first arrived in Puerto Rico. *(left: Agüeybaná greeting Ponce de Leon)* Agüeybaná's hospitality helped to maintain the peace between the Taíno and the Spaniards, a peace which was to be short-lived. Spanish authorities refused to grant to Diego Columbus (Christopher's son) privileges to all discovered land. As a result, the Crown officially appointed Juan Ponce de León governor of the island. **There was a desperate need for horses on the island.**

1510

In 1510, Captain Martin de Salazar brought some horses to Puerto Rico under the orders of Don Juan Ponce de León. Puerto Rico became a sort of strategic bridge from which horses, used in military conquests, were sent to many parts of the Latin American continent in order to claim those territories for the Spanish crown. Differences between Spaniards and Taíno Indians began. Upon Agüeybaná's death in 1510, his brother Güeybaná became the most powerful leader on the entire island. He had his doubts about the "godly" status of the Spaniards. He came up with a plan to test the perceived godly nature of the Spanish. He sent some of their tribe members to lure a Spaniard by the name of Diego Salcedo into a river and drown him. They watched over Salcedo's body to make sure that he would not resuscitate. Salcedo's death was enough to convince him and the rest of the Taíno people that the Spaniards were not gods. It is told that after they drowned Diego, they watched him for several days until they were sure that he was dead. The Taíno Indians, after learning through the drowning of Diego Salcedo, that the Spanish were mortal, revolted against Spaniards with no success. Ponce de León ordered 6,000 shot, and the survivors fled to the mountains or left the island. Shortly after, Diego Columbus won rights to all land discovered by his father after presenting his case to the courts in Madrid. King Ferdinand ordered Ponce de Leon to be replaced as governor by Diego Columbus. *(cited from http://welcome.topuertorico.org/history.shtml)*
Number of horses brought: unknown - Number of horses survived: unknown

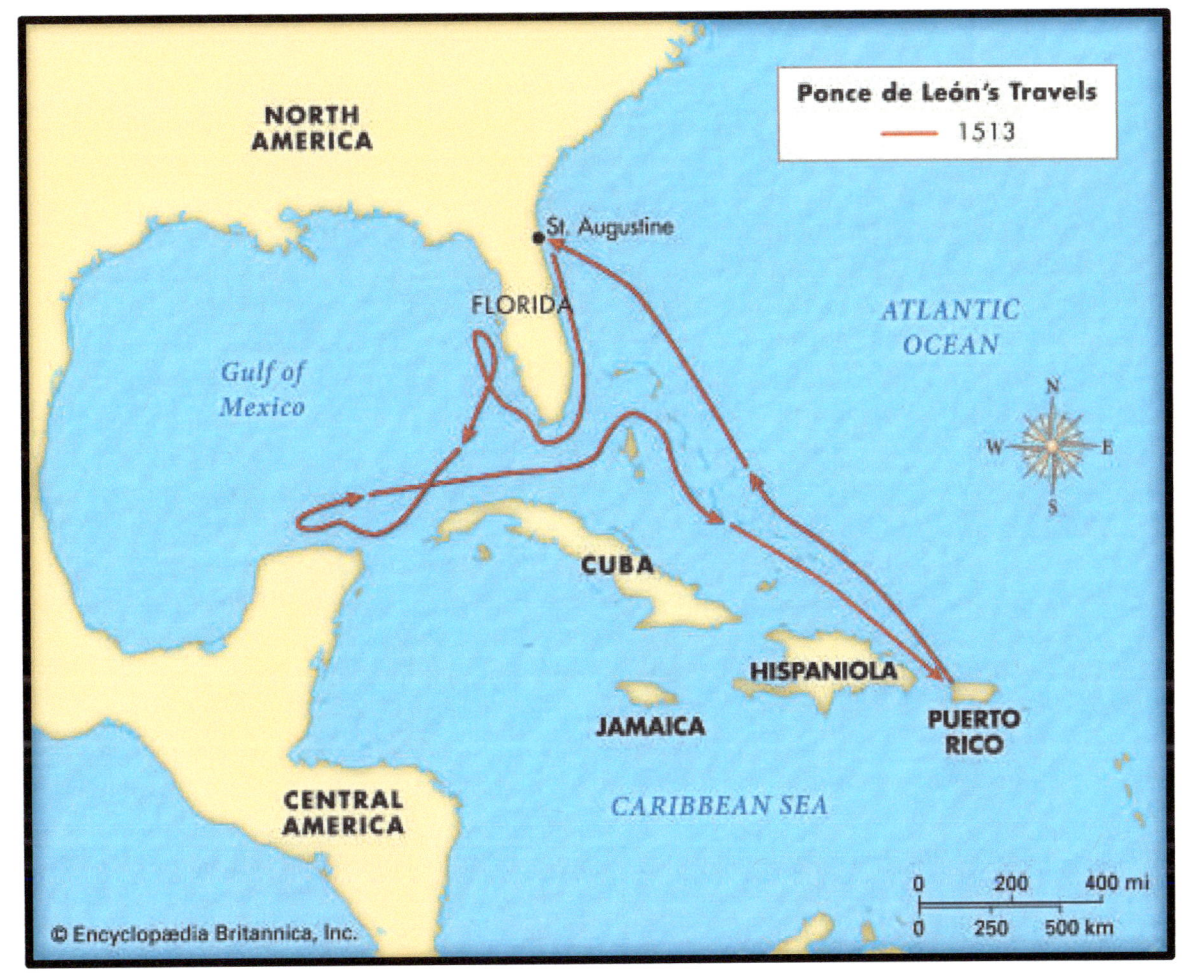

1513

Not wishing to serve Diego Columbus in Puerto Rico, Juan Ponce de León obtained title to explore the Upper Bahamas and areas to the North. He put together a crew and left Puerto Rico behind him. He sailed through the Bahamas on a Northwestern course looking for new lands and treasure. In the spring of 1513, Ponce de Leon landed on mainland Florida near what would become St. Augustine. He called it La Florida, meaning "land of flowers," and claimed it for Ferdinand, the King of Spain. Continuing down the east coast of Florida he set about giving names to the areas he encountered. He named Cape Canaveral for its currents, and the Dry Tortuga Islands for the turtles he saw there. Following the coast of Florida, Ponce de Leon and his crew sailed into the Gulf of Mexico and up the west coast of Florida. They anchored in Charlotte Harbor and hiked inland in search of fresh water.

No horses on this voyage

1518

In 1518 Baron de Lery et de St. Just was to found a colony in North America and landed at Sable Island and Canso Island off the coast of Nova Scotia. The weather was so cold that he left the horses and cattle and went back to France, probably intending to return in the spring. He never did return. The cattle and horses that De Lery brought all died or were killed by the Indians. The cattle on Sable Island also died or were removed by pirates and raiders. *(cited from https://tkmorin.wordpress.com/tag/baron-de-lery-et-de-st-just/)*

Number of horses brought: unknown - Number of horses survived: none

1519

Hernando Cortes was able to impress the Spanish administrator, Diego Velazquez, in the conquest of Cuba, and earned the position of mayor, or alcalde, of Santiago de Cuba. Cortes then convinced Velazquez to allow him to command an expedition into Mexico. Cortes was given an army of 600 men and 16 horses; they departed for the mainland on February 19, 1519. Velazquez reconsidered and tried to stop Cortes from leaving on the expedition because he was afraid that Cortes would not follow his orders if he was successful. However, his efforts were too late, and Cortes was able to leave. Cortes and his men sailed along the coast, looking for civilizations to conquer. They landed in Mexico near the town of Tabasco. Cortes, in less than 2 years, destroyed the Aztec monarchy, gained complete control of the Mexican capital of Tenochtitlan and extended his jurisdiction over most of the Aztec Empire. Cortes quickly secured the area from the natives, who were terrified by the large beasts which they had never seen before. Cortes was quoted as saying, "Next to God, we owed our victory to the horses."

Bernal Díaz, who accompanied Cortés, kept notes on all the horses, their strengths and weaknesses and who rode them. He wrote of one that was a "pinto with white stockings on his forefeet" and also a "dark roan horse with white patches on his side." In letters home to the King, the importance of the existing horses and the need for additional mounts was always emphasized. In Mexico, the black stallion Morzillo, *(left)* who was greatly loved and highly prized by Cortés, was wounded and Cortés left him with an Indian chief as the stallion could not go on. Cortés intended to return for the horse, but Cortés barely escaped the country with his life. It was over 100 years later before another set of Spanish Conquistadors traveled this land to Yucatan. The Spanish missionaries that returned to the village of the Indians that had Morzillo found something that left them in awe. Entering the last island, the missionaries came to stand before a rudely carved statue. On a platform about the height of a man, they saw the figure of a horse carved from stone. The horse sat on his quarters with his forefeet stretched before him. When Cortés left his horse all those years ago, the Indians, knowing he was ill, stabled him in a temple to care for him. Knowing nothing of this animal, they brought him chiefly banquets of almonds and raisins, fruits, chickens, all delicacies. All unsuitable for a horse! The poor horse eventually died. The Indians, fearing Cortés would return and be angry, carved the figure of El Morzillo and placed it in the temple on the lake. *(cited from http://www.oldstonehousefarm.com/PDFs/conquistadorsIII.pdf)*

Number of horses brought: 16 - Number of horses survived: unknown

1521

Juan Ponce de León returned to **Florida** with plans to build a substantial Spanish colonial settlement. In 1521, he once again sailed the Gulf of Mexico, coming ashore between what is now Charlotte Harbor and Estero Bay, perhaps near the Caloosahatchee River. Accompanying Ponce de Leon were a group of over 200 colonists made up of farmers, artisans, and priests, all ready to make Florida their home. The group unloaded large amounts of cattle, pigs, chickens and 50 horses they'd brought with them; as well as tools and seeds for agriculture. Their plan was to set up a farming colony which would trade with the islanders of Hispaniola. The Calusa tribe alerted to the presence of such a large group of incoming settlers, established an ambush. They surrounded and attacked the Spanish. A fierce battle ensued, and many Spaniards were lost. The entire group abandoned the colonization project on the spot. During the fight, Ponce de Leon was hit in the thigh by an arrow and seriously hurt. His party would make it safely back to Hispaniola, but Juan Ponce de Leon would die in Cuba from the wound which was rumored to be from a poisoned arrow. *(cited from: http://ruralfloridaliving.blogspot.com/2012/04/ponce-de-leon-and-florida-livestock.html)* Only one ship returned to Cuba. The horses that did not die must have been taken aboard this ship, as horses not disabled were very important and at this early date, very valuable. *(cited from: https://anthrosource.onlinelibrary.wiley.com/doi/pdf/10.1525/aa.1940.42.1.02a00060)*

Number of horses brought: 50 - Number of horses survived: unknown

1521-1526
A lawyer and nobleman from Spain, Lucas Vasques de Ayllón sponsored the first Spanish explorations, 3 total, of what became North Carolina. In 1521, he sent Francisco Gordillo to find a Northwest Passage. The Spaniard landed near the Cape Fear River and explored a land called Chicora between the Cape Fear and Jamestown Island. In 1524, Ayllón traveled to Chicora for his second mission, discovered the Chesapeake Bay, and offered a report to Charles V, who made the nobleman the lifetime governor of the land that he had explored. His last mission was in 1525 to 1526. Ayllón and approximately 500 to 600 colonists, including 3 monks, sailed to the New World in a convoy of 6 ships. They landed near the Cape Fear River which they called Rio Jordan but decided to go to a more respectable place. They went north and established San Miguel de Guandape. Disease, however, plagued the Spanish settlement, and the numbers dropped quickly to 150. The dead included Ayllón. Shortly afterward, Spaniards abandoned San Miguel de Guandape and approximately 80 - 100 horses.

After Ayllón's failure to establish a colony in Chicora, the emperor never again turned his eyes to the northern latitudes of North America, leaving that area to the English and the French.
Number of horses brought: unknown - Number of horses survived: 80-100

1527

The explorer and would-be colonizer **Pánfilo de Narváez** left Spain with 600 colonists and landed at Tampa Bay, **Florida** in 1527. He went inland with 300 men, 40 officers and soldiers in armor mounted upon armored horses. In Santo Domingo, 140 men deserted the expedition, and in Cuba a hurricane sank 2 of the ships, killing 50 men and several horses. Narváez remained in Cuba until late February 1528, then sailed with 5 ships and 400 followers to the region around Tampa Bay in Florida. After claiming the land for Spain, Narváez began an overland expedition in May with about 300 men. The force made a difficult and distressing march northward, continually fighting Indians, until the survivors reached the area of present-day St. Marks, Florida, near the end of July. Since the vessels from the expedition failed to come to their aid, Narváez's suffering survivors had to construct additional ships. They built 5 vessels, and in late September, 245 men sailed along the coast, hoping to reach Mexico. The ships drifted along the northern part of the Gulf of Mexico, passing Pensacola Bay and the mouth of the Mississippi River. As the journey progressed, the boats were gradually lost, and at about the beginning of November 1528, Narváez disappeared when his own vessel was suddenly blown out to sea. Only 4 men survived the expedition. *(cited from: https://www.britannica.com/biography/Panfilo-de-Narvaez)* There are very explicit statements that all the horses were slaughtered for food, the last one on September 22. *(cited from: https://anthrosource.onlinelibrary.wiley.com/doi/pdf/10.1525/aa.1940.42.1.02a00060)*

Number of horses brought: unknown - Number of horses survived: none

1531-1535

Francisco Pizarro arrived in present-day northern **Peru** late in 1531 with a small force of about 180 men and 37 horses. Taking advantage of a civil war, he and his compatriots, including **Diego de Almgro**, toppled the ruler, Atahualpa, in 1532. Once the Inca Empire was pacified, Almagro and Pizarro began having troubles. The Crown's division of Peru was vague, and the wealthy city of Cuzco fell under Almagro's jurisdiction, but the powerful Pizarro and his brothers held it. Almagro went north and participated in the conquest of Quito, but the north was not as rich, and Almagro seethed at what he saw as Pizarro schemed to cut him out of the New World loot. Charles V gave Almagro a grant extending two hundred leagues south of Francisco Pizarro's. Pizarro and Almagro concluded a new contract on 12 June 1535, in which they agreed to share future discoveries equally. Diego raised an expedition for Chile, expecting it would lead to even greater riches than they had found in Peru. Almagro left Peru for **Chile** in 1535, taking with him 200 Spanish horses and many Indian burden bearers. The expedition was very difficult, and a failure and he eventually returned to Peru. **Number of horses brought to Peru: 37 Number of horses survived: unknown   Number of horses brought to Chile: 200 Number of horses survived: unknown**

1535

Pedro de Mendoza brought horses from Cadiz, Spain, to the Rio de la Plata, **Buenos Aires**. In 1540, the hostility of the native populace forced the Spaniards to abandon Buenos Aires. Journal records state that all the horses that were brought either died of starvation or were eaten since the people were also starving. Legend says that Mendoza's horses reproduced into great herds on the pampas, but there is no proof for this. Buenos Aires was abandoned from 1541 to 1580. There are far more probabilities of the introduction of livestock from the west side of the pampa than directly from the Old World to the east. Besides traveling with Mendoza and, later, with Cabeza de Vaca, horses had gone from Peru to Chile, from Peru to the numerous cities of the back-country province of Tucuman, from Peru and Charcas to Paraguay. While Buenos Aires lay waste for 40 years, Chile and Tucuman were being settled. *(cited from https://anthrosource.onlinelibrary.wiley.com/ doi/pdf/10.1525/aa.1939.41.1.02a00100)*
Number of horses brought: unknown - Number of horses survived: none

1538

Hernando de Soto's expedition traveled throughout Florida north through the Carolinas, into Tennessee, south into Alabama, west into Mississippi, Arkansas and finally Texas. DeSoto sailed from Spain with 9 vessels and 600 men, in April 1538, for Santiago, Cuba. After a short delay in Cuba, he left Havana May 18, 1539, for Florida where he established a camp near Tampa Bay. He came ashore with 237 horses. He traveled on, leaving 50 footmen and 30 horses as a garrison. The men and horses of this garrison joined him later at Apalache. From the camp near Tampa Bay, he set out, August 1, 1539, on his westward exploring expedition, taking with him 550 men and 200 horses. Of these 200 horses, 12 were killed in what is now Alabama; 70 were wounded, and 50 perished at the Chickasaw battle in the now state of Mississippi. DeSoto reached the east bank of the Mississippi in May 1541, with about 98 horses, including 30 that joined him at Apalache. Those that survived were ferried across the Mississippi never to return. *(cited from https://anthrosource.onlinelibrary.wiley.com/doi/pdf/10.1525/aa.1940.42.1.02a00060)* **Number of horses brought: 237 - Number of horses survived: 98**

1540-42

After the failure of the expedition of Diego de Almagro in 1536, the lands to the south of Peru had remained unexplored. Pedro de Valdivia asked governor Francisco Pizarro for permission to complete the conquest of that territory. Valdivia began his expedition in 1540. At first, Valdivia was successful in his efforts to deal benevolently with the native population, but this peaceful coexistence did not last long. Indian trouble forced him to send back to Peru for reinforcements. At the time he reported having 50 mares in Chile. Alonso de Monroy offered to go in search of relief. Valdivia accepted the offer, and in January 1542 Monroy left for Peru with the best horses, along with 5 company soldiers. When Monroy and his band set out in this quest for aid, each man carried as baggage 4 spare shoes for his horse and a bag of a hundred nails. Captured by the Indians, Monroy and one companion were left alive to teach their masters how to ride the horses they had so newly acquired. They remained captive for 3 months until they were given the opportunity to flee and continue on their way. *(cited from http://www.biografiadechile.cl/detalle.php?IdContenido=373&IdCategoria=8&IdArea=35&TituloPagina=Historia%20de%20Chile and https://anthrosource.onlinelibrary.wiley.com/doi/pdf/10.1525/aa.1939.41.1.02a00100)* **Number of horses brought: 50 - Number of horses survived: unknown**

1540

Francisco Vásquez de Coronado approached Texas from the west. He started from Mexico City, mustered his expedition at Compostela, and marched north to **Arizona**, then east to **New Mexico** and on to **Texas**. In 1541 he approached the plains with a force estimated at 1,500 people, 1,000 horses, 500 cattle, and 5,000 sheep. He spent more than 5 months on the plains where he lost many horses. Some were gored by buffalo, some fell into a ravine during a buffalo chase. A few might have strayed away without their loss being noted by the chronicler, and it is conceivable that a stallion and a mare might have strayed off together. The muster rolls of the expedition list 2 mares starting out from Compostela, and there might have been a few more not listed. Spanish explorers and buffalo hunters from the later Santa Fe settlements found no wild horses of any kind in this area before 1700. It seems reasonable, then, that any such strays were wiped out by bad water, storms, accidents, and predators such as the wolf and cougar. *(cited from: https://www.americanheritage.com/content/how-indian-got-horse)*

Number of horses brought: 1000 - Number of horses survived: unknown

1545 - 1554

Francisco de Villagra went to **Chile** in 1545, in response to a request of Valdivia for aid, and brought with him 400 horses. One of Valdivia's letters to Charles V tells of the horses already stolen from him by wily Araucanians. Valdivia was eventually defeated by Lautaro in 1553. Chief Lautaro *(below)* had served as head groom to Valdivia. The city hastily called on Francisco de Villagra to take command of the country and organize resistance. Villagra was defeated in 1554. Of the 5 cities founded in the south of the country by the first conqueror of Chile only the 2 near the coast, Imperial and Valdivia remained standing, and, of the 3 forts of Araucania, not one remained. The Indians began their wholesale and systematic collection of the Spanish horses. Through the many Andean passes, these, newly Indian, horses were driven to the security of the plains where they ran wild and where Pampa Indian allies also came to learn of the value of horses for food and for easy travel. The early date of the introduction of horses into Chile, the wholesale destruction of South Chilean settlements in the 1550s and the fact that considerable numbers of horses were turned loose upon the pampa in a region where, running north and east in search of better pasture, they would logically approach the plains of Buenos Aires, offering a far more satisfactory explanation for the mysterious appearance of the wild herds of 1580 than any mythical Mendozan ancestors. *(cited from: https://anthrosource.onlinelibrary.wiley.com/doi/pdf/10.1525/aa.1939.41.1.02a00100)*

Number of horses brought: 400 - Number of horses survived: unknown

1543 - 1573

Parallel with the settlement in Paraguay and Chile was that of the old colonial province of Tucuman, Argentina. From the time of the "Gran entrada" of Diego de Rojas in 1543 and the first colonizing expedition of Nunez de Prado in 1550, conquering Spaniards toured the land of Tucuman, and settling Spaniards founded town after town. Spanish horses were essential to the success of these Spanish conquerors. The extensiveness of this introduction of stock is evident from the fact that as early as 1566, 14 years before the second founding of Buenos Aires, 120 armed men and 500 "spare" horses had been mustered in Tucuman to go exploring for the mysterious and romantically lost land of the Caesars. Roberto Levillier published the several "service records" of the town government of these inland cities. There is no more graphic portrayal of the early and extended development of the livestock industry on the Argentine plains than this account of colonial inter-city aid. The city of Santiago del Estero sent 1000 horses in aid of the foundation of Cordoba in 1573, and similar aid was given at the founding of Londres, Cordoba de Calchaqui, Cainete, Talavera. Gonzalo de Abreu received over 1000 horses for the founding of San Clemente; Hernando de Lerma, in the founding of Salta, received 2000 horses, and a proportionate number of cows, goats, sheep. *(cited from: https://anthrosource.onlinelibrary.wiley.com/doi/pdf/10.1525/aa.1939.41.1.02a00100)* **Number of horses mentioned in records: 1000s**

1559

Another expedition from Mexico, with the definite aim of colonizing Santa Elena on the Carolina coast, was undertaken by Tristan de Luna who, with others, began extensive preparations in 1558, though it did not actually sail till June 11, 1559. That this was no light undertaking may be judged from the fact that 13 vessels were required to transport 1000 camp followers, men, women, children, negroes and Indians, 500 soldiers, half foot and half horse, with 240 horses, "the latter," as the Chronicler relates, "by no means the least important;" but, "only 130 survived the long voyage" to be disembarked at Mobile Bay, where they were sent overland to Pensacola Bay. Like most of the early expeditions trials and tribulations harassed the men, women, and horses from the start. Starvation faced the soldiers so that at one time they were reduced to eating the trappings of their horses and the leather of their shields. By August 1560 there were "only about 50 or 60 horses and these are in such condition that it happens that when our people go out to hunt, they come back on foot all tired out, the horses being unable to carry them because they have eaten no corn for a year." "Opinion of the Captains" to Luna written in 1560 states as follows: "The horses and mules which are here, which must number about 50, are so thin and weak from eating no corn for so long, that if any of us go hunting from this camp on them, it always happens that within half a league from here they become exhausted, and those who go on them have to leave them behind and come back carrying the saddles on their shoulders." Some of the horses that did not die from exhaustion and starvation were slaughtered, so that horse meat was publicly weighed out to give rations to the people. *(cited from: https://anthrosource.onlinelibrary.wiley.com/doi/pdf/10.1525/aa.1940.42.1.02a00060)*

Number of horses brought: 240 - Number of horses survived: most likely none

1573

Juan Ortiz de Zárate, explorer and conquistador, landed his expedition at the mouth of the Rio Plata at what is now Colonia, Uruguay in 1573. His purpose was to populate the area, found cities and introduce cattle and horses. Some journals report that he brought 300 horses. He and Juan de Garay defeated the Charrúa Indians. Zárate assumed governorship in Asunción where he held the office until 1575. *(cited from: https://www.euskalkazeta.com/basques-in-the-americas-1492-to-1592/ and https://anthrosource.onlinelibrary.wiley.com/doi/pdf/10.1525/aa.1940.42.1.02a00060)*

Number of horses brought: 300 - Number of horses survived: unknown

1601

The Indians at Buenos Aires were relatively peaceful folk; long before 1580 they had been quite thoroughly subdued. They never became equestrian. Buenos Aires only began her real Indian troubles with the invasions of the horse-riding Pehuenches *(left)* and their kindred Araucanians from the west. Droves of horses had been allowed to run wild after the Chilean massacres of the 50s. They were herded across the South Chilean valley passes, set free in the security of the plains. Gradually they drifted down into the pampa. Taught by Araucanian kinsmen traders, the Pehuenches learned to ride, and then the wild Indian began his pursuit of the wild horse he craved. So successful were they in these thefts that by 1601 the Chilean Indians were reported as being able to muster 2,000, 3,000 and even 4,000 horses while the Spaniards had difficulty in collecting a mere 600.

(cited from: https://anthrosource.onlinelibrary.wiley.com/doi/pdf/10.1525/aa.1939.41.1.02a00100)

1604

M. L'Escarbot, a French lawyer, brought several horses to Acadia (known today as the Maritimes in Canada). Some sources say that King Henry IV provided these horses. *(cited from: The Wild Horse Dilemma: Conflicts and Controversies of the Atlantic Coast Herds, p. 206)*

Number of horses brought: unknown - Number of horses survived: unknown

1609

"Six mares and two horses" were loaded onto the Blessing in Plymouth, England, in May 1609 for a three-month voyage to Jamestown. When a wounded John Smith returned to England for medical treatment in the fall of 1609, Chief Powhatan ordered his warriors to lay siege to James Fort. The 300 colonists trapped within began to starve to death. As the winter dragged on, they ate rats, cats, dogs, snakes "or what vermin or carrion we could light on." *(above)* In this "starving time" winter they even butchered the horses brought from England the summer before. Sir Ferdinando Wenman was the "Generall of the Horse" in the Jamestown colony and also Master of the Ordnance at James Fort — a knight who was responsible for Jamestown's arms and armor. But Wenman himself did not survive the "starving time" and died in 1610 at the age of 34. *(cited from: https://historicjamestowne.org/selected-artifacts/horse-bones-2/)*

Number of horses brought: 8 - Number of horses survived: none

1611

Sir Thomas Dale was sent by the Virginia Company of London as Deputy Governor or "High Marshall of Virginia." He landed in **Jamestown** on May 19, 1611, with new settlers, livestock, and supplies including 17 horses. The Governor and the Plantation owners imported multiple shipments of the Hobby Horse *(left: 1581 etching from John Derricke's "The Image of Irelande")* directly from Ireland. Virginia and Ireland had a trade agreement, and later a treaty wherein Ireland supplied all the cattle, sheep and horses for the colony. Horses in the Virginia colony were almost exclusively of Irish Hobby descent. The last shipment of Hobbies to Virginia was in 1666 when Sir Thomas Southwell gathered the remnants of the old Desmond Stud (a stallion and 4 mares) and shipped them to Virginia. *(cited from: www.sport-horse-breeder.com)*

Number of horses brought: 17 - Number of horses survived: unknown

1613

Captain Thomas Argall (who had kidnapped Pocahontas in April of 1613) sailed 500 miles to **Port Royal, Nova Scotia**. He destroyed the French settlement and brought horses back to Jamestown. These horses were probably the best French bloodlines of the time and most likely were of Iberian descent. *(cited from: The Wild Horse Dilemma: Conflicts and Controversies of the Atlantic Coast Herds, p. 206)*

Number of horses brought: unknown - Number of horses survived: unknown

1620

Until 1624 the **Virginia Company** was the principal source for imported livestock to the colonies. In 1620 a census counted 11 horses in the colony. Horses were allowed to range freely. Horses often damaged crops. In 1643 the Virginia Assembly ruled that colonists were required to fence crops. Writings and journals declared the horses to be "as good as we have in England" and "of an excellent race." *(cited from: The Wild Horse Dilemma: Conflicts and Controversies of the Atlantic Coast Herds, p. 207)* **In 1649 there were 200 horses in Virginia**

1620

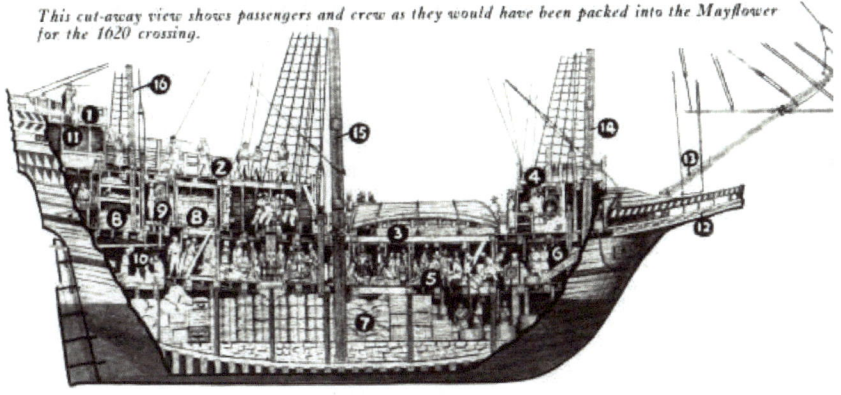

This cut-away view shows passengers and crew as they would have been packed into the Mayflower for the 1620 crossing.

KEY TO DRAWING
1. Poop deck.
2. Half deck.
3. Upper deck.
4. Forecastle.
5. Main deck where most of the Pilgrims were housed.
6. Crew's quarters.
7. Large hold.
8. Special cabins.
9. Helmsman with whipstaff controlling the tiller.
10. Tiller room.
11. Captain's cabin.
12. Beak.
13. Bowsprit.
14. Foremast.
15. Mainmast.
16. Mizzen mast.

The Mayflower departed Plymouth, England on September June 16, 1620. The 100-foot ship had 102 passengers and a crew of 30 - 40 in extremely cramped conditions. The Mayflower arrived in Plymouth Bay on December 20, 1620. In April 1621, Governor Carver collapsed while working in the fields on a hot day. He died a few days later. The settlers of Plymouth then chose William Bradford as the new governor, a position which he retained off-and-on for the rest of his life. The Pilgrims did not bring any large livestock animals with them on the Mayflower. In fact, the only animals known with certainty to have come on the Mayflower were two dogs, an English Mastiff, and an English spaniel who is mentioned on a couple of occasions in the Pilgrims' journals. Although not specifically mentioned, it seems likely that they had with them some chickens because chicken broth was given by Mayflower passenger Edward Winslow to the Wampanoag sachem Massasoit when he was sick in early 1622; and it is also likely they brought some pigs. In 1623, Emmanual Altham visited Plymouth and reported there were six goats, fifty pigs, and many chickens. The first record of the actual presence of a horse in Plymouth seems to be in 1632. Governor John Winthrop, of the Massachusetts Bay colony, describes in his diary a journey made to Plymouth in that year, partly by boat and partly on foot, and states that on his return he was sent a part of the way on " the Governor's mare " as a mark of special respect. As to the number of horses in Plymouth at that time, however, no information can be gleaned from Bradford's narrative, for he, in common with other writers of the period, uses the term cattle more or less indiscriminately to cover any sort of livestock, including horses.
(cited from: http://mayflowerhistory.com/livestock/ and https://archive.org/stream/horseraisinginco00phil/horseraisinginco00phil_djvu.txt)

Number of horses brought: none

1624

The Dutch founded New Amsterdam in 1609. As early as 1624 Dutch horses were being imported from Ultrect in Holland into the area. In 1635, 2 shiploads of Dutch horses arrived in Salem, Massachusetts and were sold for higher prices than horses that arrived from England. In 1664 they abandoned the area to the English, and the name was changed to New York. The Dutch horses remained and continued to be sold and advertised as "Dutch trotters" well into the late 1700s. *(cited from: http://www.fhana.com/the-fresian-horse/friesian-history and The Horse of America in His Derivation, History and Development pp)*

Number of horses brought: unknown - Number of horses survived: unknown

1629-1630

At this time, it was illegal to leave England without the permission of the King. On March 4th, 1629, the Massachusetts Bay Company was given its Charter by Charles I. On August 26th, 1629, a dozen shareholders from Boston, Lincolnshire, including **John Winthrop and Thomas Dudley** signed a contract to "inhabit and develop New England." Although it was a commercial company, the leading promoters of it were Puritans intent on creating a church free from outside interference. When King Charles granted a colonial charter to the Massachusetts Bay Company, the document failed to specify that the governor and officers of the company had to remain in England. The Puritan stockholders took advantage of this omission and moved the whole company and its colonial government flock, stock, and barrel to America. The richer Massachusetts Bay colony seems to have been better supplied than the colony at Plymouth. The fleet that arrived with **Francis Higginson** and its numerous settlers in the year 1629 brought over also a considerable number of horses and cattle, 115 head in all among which were 13 horses. In the following year, the ships that brought over Governor Winthrop and the second group of 700 colonists had on board 240 cows and about 60 horses, as is learned from Winthrop's letters. Some of these animals died while in route and it is not certain just how many were added to the stock of the colony, but among the horses that survived there were both mares and stallions. They landed in Salem. *(left)* There was an existing settlement at Salem, started in about 1626, populated by a few hundred Puritans and who were governed by John Endicott. The new colonists eventually settled in what is now **Boston.** Despite the hardship of the early colonists, they found the new land to be very favorable for livestock. This feature of the country is frequently mentioned in letters written to friends in England by the early settlers and in the accounts of travelers. Francis Higginson, writing in 1629, describes the abundance of grass "which groweth everywhere, both verie thicke, verie longe, and verie high in divers places" and in regard to livestock he records "it do prosper and like well this countrie." *(cited from: http://www.iboston.org/mcp.php?pid=taleOfTwoBostons and https://archive.org/stream/horseraisinginco00phil/horseraisinginco00phil_djvu.txt)*

Number of horses brought: 73 - Number of horses survived: unknown

1633

In England, Thomas Hooker was forced into exile by the persecution exacted on the Puritans by Archbishop William Laud. He traveled first to Holland and then, following the example of the Mayflower Pilgrims, made the holy pilgrimage to Massachusetts Bay in 1633. It wasn't very long at all before Hooker was in conflict with the Massachusetts Bay Colony. He disagreed with Winthrop over who could take part in the civil government. This conflict for Hooker was unresolvable. In 1634, Hooker and his congregation applied for permission to remove to Connecticut. Governor Winthrop's Journal, dated 5 October 1635, states: "about sixty men, women, and little children, went by land toward Connecticut with their cows, horses and swine, and after a tedious and difficult journey arrived safe there." Hooker's wife was too ill to walk and so was carried on a horse-drawn litter. *(above)* Upon their arrival, they settled north of the Dutch. They originally called their new home Newtown but changed it to Hartford.
(cited from: josfamilyhistory.com/stories/hooker.htm)
Number of horses brought: unknown - Number of horses survived: unknown

1650 - 1670

Both Bradford and Winthrop kept track in their journals of the number of horses arriving. For instance, in 1635 Winthrop also speaks of the arrival of a Dutch vessel with "27 Flanders mares and 3 horses." New England's dependence on horses lasted for about 20 years. By the 1650s New England's livestock population was growing on its own. Based on tax records, the ratio of livestock to households averaged between 3:1 and 6:1.
(cited from: Creatures of Empire: How Domestic Animals ,Transformed Early America By Virginia DeJohn Anderson, chapter 3)

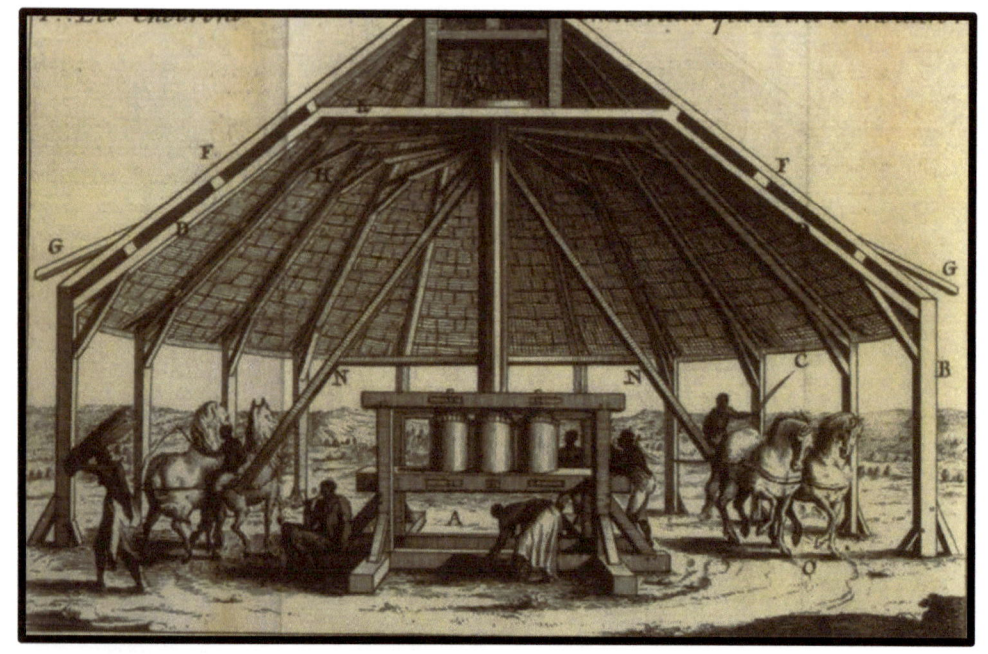

1660

(and continuing for 100+ years)

The rapid development of the British sugar islands called for great quantities of supplies to carry on the work of the plantations. During the period between 1649 and 1658, the importations of English horses were especially numerous. In those years there are recorded in the British Colonial Papers 48 permits for such shipments, for a total of more than 1,900 horses. England continued to send horses until as late as 1667 but the levying in 1654 of an export duty of 20 shillings a head cut down the numbers considerably and hastened the shift in the trade by which New England at length became almost the sole source of supply for the islands. In that region, there was no export duty except in Massachusetts Bay, where it was the only sixpence, and the cost of transportation was much less because of the shorter distance, which also resulted in much smaller losses in transit. Horses were so abundant in New England that they were exported from New England to the other continental colonies. The main demand that resulted in the exportation of New England horses came from the sugar plantations in the West Indies where horses were needed for draft purposes. *(above)* The New England colonies became the accepted source of supply for this demand from the sugar islands, resulting chiefly from the fact that they were the only ones which possessed a surplus of horses at the time when the demand first began to make itself felt. In most of the other colonies, there was an actual scarcity of horses, as in Virginia. As the settlement of New England grew, it was very soon discovered that there were certain areas in Rhode Island and in Connecticut which were much better adapted to the raising of livestock of all kinds than the region first settled. These more favored areas were found mainly in the upper valley of the Connecticut River, along with the shore of Long Island Sound, and about Narragansett Bay in Rhode Island. Shipping of horses to the islands was a very important source of income to the New England colonies for a hundred years. Between 1771 and 1774 the record of the Secretary of Customs in London noted that 7,130 horses were shipped from North America to the British Islands. Certain areas were specialized for breeding horses. This was the case, for example, on Fisher's Island which was given over almost entirely to animal husbandry. Also, in the Connecticut River Valley, the region around Windsor seems to have been another such center. But by far the most extensive and important of these specialized areas was to be found in the Narragansett district of Rhode Island. The wealth of the area increased steadily up to the time of the Revolution. *(cited from: https://archive.org/stream/horseraisinginco00phil/horseraisinginco00phil_djvu.txt)*

1665

In 1665, **Louis XIV** sent a French garrison, the Carignan-Salières Regiment, *(left)* to **Quebec**. With them, he sent the first horses to New France to be distributed among the military officers of the Carignan-Salieres regiment, government officials, and religious communities of the colony. The first royal horses destined for the New World left Le Havre on the ship Le Marie Therese on May 10, 1665. After 9 perilous and stormy weeks at sea, 2 stallions and 12 mares set hoof on the shores of New France at Tadoussac on July 16th. Another shipment of 15 royal horses arrived on September 25, 1667, with similar shipments reported in 1668, and 1669. In 1670, a stallion and 12 more mares arrived to be distributed among the gentlemen of New France. A final shipment of 13 horses arrived in 1671, for a total of 81 horses. In 1671, the King's Chief Steward, Jean Talon, wrote Louis the 14th to explain that no more shipments would be required since there were enough horses in New France to meet the colony's needs. *(cited from: http://marielynnhammond.com/LegacyCanadians/1098845.htm)*

Number of horses brought: 81 - Number of horses survived: unknown – records show that horses did reproduce

1665

The first race-course in North America was built on the Salisbury Plains - now known as the Hempstead Plains - of **Long Island, New York** in 1665. The present site of Belmont Park is on the Western edge of the Hempstead Plains. In 1665, the first horse racing meet in North America was held at this race-course called "Newmarket" after the famous track in England. These early races were matched events between 2 or 3 horses and were run in heats at a distance of 3 or 4 miles; a horse had to complete in at least 2 heats to be judged the winner. *(cited from: http://virginiahistoryseries.org)*

1669

By 1669 there were so many wild horses in **Virginia** that further importation was prohibited. Stallions were to be gelded if caught and laws were passed for horse owners to reimburse farmers for damaged crops. *(cited from: The Wild Horse Dilemma: Conflicts and Controversies of the Atlantic Coast Herds, p. 210)*

1674

Horse races were held near **Richmond in Enrico County, now Henrico County, Virginia,** in 1674. Forward-thinking Virginia colonists began to improve upon the speed of horses by introducing some of the best early imports from England into their local bloodlines. Horse racing has always been popular in Virginia, especially during Colonial times when one-on-one matches took place down village streets, country lanes and across level pastures. *(cited from: http://virginiahistoryseries.org)*

1681

Jesuit Missionary Eusebio Francisco Kino *(below)* arrived in the New World in 1681. Father Kino began leaving bands of 20 to 30 of his Spanish "mission horses" at each small settlement that he founded or visited throughout the **Pimería Alta (present-day Arizona and Sonora, Mexico).** Using Spanish horses he obtained from missions to the south, Kino's breeding ranch at Mission Nuestra Señora de los Dolores in Sonora produced a horse that could carry a rider over 60 miles of rough terrain in a single day. Kino's horses quickly adapted to the temperature extremes and punishing terrain and could survive by feeding on the sparse vegetation of the arid Sonoran Desert. *(cited from: http://padrekino.com/kino-legacy/horseman/)*

1730

The first Thoroughbred horse imported into the American Colonies was Bulle Rock who was imported in 1730 by **Samuel Gist** of **Hanover County**, **Virginia**. He was 21 years old and had been a successful racehorse in Britain. He was sired by Darley Arabian *(right)* one of the first three stallions, who between them, would become the progenitors of every living Thoroughbred. By 1800, Bulle Rock was followed by a succession of 338 other imported Thoroughbreds. *(cited from http://virginiahistoryseries.org)* America's first jockey club, composed of wealthy horse owners and breeders, was organized in **Charleston, South Carolina,** in 1734. Five years later, Williamsburg's Virginia Gazette heralded a race in which eight horses competed over a one-mile course, with a trumpeter's blast signaling the start and the winner earning 40 shillings.

America was a divided sprawl of Quakers and Puritans, Catholics and Dutch, Yankees and Southerners, Tories and slaves. More than a million people resided in what was still, in some ways, a brutal frontier, with disease claiming many children, Indians attacking the fringes, and pickpockets and horse thieves being put to death. But a sophisticated society was rapidly evolving as every year ships delivered more people and culture from England. There was theater to enjoy, newspapers to read and postal routes for the mail. The population was still too far-flung and dissimilar to agree on much, especially independence, an idea just beginning to percolate. But colonists from Rhode Island to the Carolinas could all agree that nothing was more heavenly than a fast horse. A few 2nd and 3rd generation Virginia planters were able to accumulate large land holdings. They built large plantations and bred horses. Some of these famous plantations included: William Byrd II- Westover *(right – built in the 1730s)*, William Fitzhugh – Bedford, Ralph Wormley - Rosegill, Thomas Lee - Stratford Hall, John Carter – Shirley, Governor Beverley - Green Spring, Laurence Washington (George Washington) - Mount Vernon, John Tayloe - Mt. Airy, Thomas Jefferson - Monticello, George Mason - Gunston Hall, Thomas Lord Fairfax – Greenway, Carter Burwell - Carter's Grove. *(cited from: https://www.smithsonianmag.com/history/off-to-the-races-2266179/ and http://virginiahistoryseries.org)*

1740
A Portuguese man, **Joao Francisco,** moved to an area in **Brazil** south of Minas during the 1740s and formed the Hacienda Campo Alegre. One of Joao's sons, the Baron of Alfenas, was presented with an Alter-Real stallion called Sublime by Dom Pedro I, Emperor of Brazil. Sublime was mated with mostly Spanish Jennet mares, and also with some Criollo and Andalusian mares.

1750
By the 1750s, all the **tribes** of the **Great Plains** had horses. They had become experts at raising, training and riding horses. Each Indian of the Great Plains could ride a horse by the age of five. As an adult, a young man would have a special horse for work. Another horse would be trained for hunting, and another would be trained for war. An Indian warrior's success depended upon how closely he and his horses worked together. George Catlin was an artist who traveled a great deal in the early American west. He painted many beautiful pictures of American Indians. Mr. Catlin said the Plains Indian was the greatest horse rider the world has ever known. He said the moment an Indian rider laid a hand on his horse he became part of the animal.
(Right: Buffalo Hunt by George Catlin 1844)
(cited from:
http://www.manythings.org/voa/history/4.html)

1775

At the outbreak of the Revolutionary War, most of the British troops in the American colonies were billeted in Boston. There was no cavalry, few field guns, and no field supply system. The shortage of cavalry in the Revolutionary War was a major drawback for the British. In October 1775, the British undertook a remarkable effort to supply the army in Boston with enough fresh quality provisions to last through the winter. The firm of Mure, Son & Atkinson was contracted to furnish enough fresh food and livestock to fill 36 ships. Only 13 ships eventually made it to Boston. Only the preserved food (sauerkraut, vinegar, and porter, a type of beer) survived intact. Most of the other provisions were rotten or damaged. Out of 856 horses shipped, only 532 survived the voyage. Shipment of many commodities from Britain was deemed impracticable, so the army resorted to local sources for fresh food, fodder, and transportation. This had a great impact on the course of the war; when supply reserves dropped below the 2-month level, which they often did, British generals stopped thinking about offensive action and began to plan evacuation. To have any hope of victory, the British had to seek out the rebel army and defeat it. Yet far too often their soldiers were forced to sit and wait or, worse, to evacuate a position, garrison, or city that had already been gained through difficult fighting. The effect that logistics deficiencies had on these decisions to wait or pull back is undeniable. The convoy of 36 ships marked the last time that Britain attempted to ship fresh food and livestock to its army. *(cited from: http://www.almc.army.mil/alog/issues/sepoct99/ms409.htm) (left: "Evacuation Day" – The British leave Boston)*

The American Revolution is the last recorded time that horses were brought to the Americas in large numbers.

1800s

The horse, one of the most remarkable prime movers on the planet, pretty much ruled 19th-century urban life and rural culture in both Europe and North America. Until the 19th century, horses remained largely a status animal that signified wealth. The well-to-do could afford horses and used them for personal transportation, but most people just walked. The poor harnessed the sturdy and practical ox to a wagon for longer travels. Most 19th century cities were no wider than 2 miles and highly walkable. Before long, however, the horse became the backbone of 19th-century life. North Americans employed 4,000,000 horses in 1840 for agricultural work and travel. By 1900 they were harnessing more than 24 million horses, a six-fold increase, to plow fields, as well as pull street trolleys, drays, brewery wagons, city vehicles, omnibuses, and carriages. For every 3 people there trod 1 working horse in the United States. *(cited from: https://thetyee.ca/News/2013/03/06/Horse-Dung-Big-Shift/)*

BRING ON THE BREEDS!
Mares and Foals by George Stubbs 1762

Types of Horses That Came to the Americas

Explorers and settlers brought many types of horses with them to the New World. The types of horses were most often the type used in the area they came from. Importing horses for a purpose and breeding for a purpose did not begin until the Americas were well established.

Types of Horses by Country of Origin

Dutch Horses

Dutch horses *(left: today's Friesians are descendants of Dutch horses that came to America)* were about 14.1 hands with good bone and muscle; more so than the English horses. Based on records of sales from the 1600s the Dutch horses brought more money than other horses. In 1842 Justin Morgan, Jr. wrote that his father referred to Figure (the horse that was the progenitor of the Morgan breed) as "the Dutch horse…. of the best blood." The Dutch horses were not known to be saddle horses. Therefore, they were likely not amblers. *(cited from: The Horse of America in His Derivation, History and Development. p 374)*

French Horses

Horses were sent to Canada from the Royal Stables of Louis XIV. (*right: Louis XIV*) Horses were divided by type in the Royal stables; carriage, hunting and riding school. Their coats were of all types of colors, and three-quarters of them came from abroad: England, Ireland, Spain, North Africa and northern Europe. In his "Brief Description of Versailles," Félibien wrote that "in the stables at Versailles alone, you see what you could not hope to see anywhere else except on long journeys, an admirable and elite collection of horses". The horses in the stables were chosen with care, and their beauty and the quality of their dressage amazed visitors. Most likely quality horses were sent to the Americas. *(cited from: http://en.chateauversailles.fr/discover/history/horses-versailles#the-king's-horses, Image:*

English and Irish Horses

In early England nags, jades, hackneys and draught-horses powered the English economy. Tudor and Stuart monarchs took the lead in improving the quality of the stock by importing Barbs, Turkomans, Neapolitans and other foreign horses; by cross-breeding these with native stock; and by setting more exacting standards at the royal studs. Likewise, the landed classes emulated the Crown; they imported foreign horses and used them for breeding purposes. *(cited from: Horse and Man in Early Modern England, pp 1-16)*

The first horses that came to the New World from England were persistently small, and many possessed a natural pacing gait. This possible progenitor is to be found in the Irish Hobbies, a type of small, hardy, wild ponies existing in Ireland during the first part of the 17th century. *(left: Histoire du Roy d'Angleterre Richard 1399 showing Art Mor McMurrough, king of Leinster "rush down a hill faster than a deer or hare:")* These horses were in great demand in England for saddle purposes and were exported in such quantities that they are said to have become practically extinct in Ireland before the year 1634. They were well known in England, and their natural pacing gait made them especially desirable in any place where travel was of necessity on horseback; it is not at all improbable, therefore, that some of them found their way to New England, where they would have been especially serviceable. *(cited from: https://archive.org/stream/horseraisinginco00phil/horseraisinginco00phil_djvu.txt)*

Spanish Horses

Horses brought by the Spanish were a combination of Iberian horses, African Barbs, and Spanish Jennets.

The Iberian Peninsula of southwest Europe contains the countries of Spain, Portugal, Andorra, and Gibraltar, as well as a very small portion of France. The Iberian Horse *(right)* is an ancient breed. Cave paintings of its ancestors, estimated to be 20,000 years old, have been found on the Iberian Peninsula, where Spain and Portugal are located today. Ancient Greeks and Romans revered the Iberian Horse for his courage, agility, and beauty, and the knights of medieval Europe charged into battle astride their broad backs. *(cited from: https://www.equisearch.com/articles/spanish-horse-breeds)*

The Barb is an ancient breed that was established in the Fertile Crescent of Middle Asia. *(left: Moorish knight and horse, drawing by Jacopo Ligozzi 1547-1627)* The fast and agile Barb was a favored mount for the Berbers. In fact, the animal draws its name from this group of "barbarous" people. The Barb was originally a prized warhorse, which explains its worldwide distribution. As the Berbers conquered new lands, the horses left behind were bred with native stock. Barbs were most plentiful along the coast of Africa, and the Moors used them to invade Spain. The horses were later taken by the Conquistadors to the New World. *(cited from: http://horsechannel.com/horse-breeds/profiles/barb-horse-horse-breed.aspx)*

The Jennet *(right)* was a type of horse more than a distinct breed. The term "Jennet" was in regular use during the Middle Ages to refer to a specific type of horse, often gaited. It was noted for a smooth naturally ambling gait, compact and well-muscled build, and a good disposition. The Jennet was an ideal light riding horse.

Types of Horses by Way of Going

Gaits of the Horse

Horses move naturally with four basic gaits: the 4 beat walk, which averages 4.0 mph, the 2 beat trot or jog, which averages 8.1 to 12 mph, and the leaping gaits known as the canter or lope, a 3 beat gait that is 12 to 15 mph and the gallop, a 4 beat movement which averages 25 to 30 mph.

Besides these basic gaits, some horses perform a 2 beat pace, instead of the trot. The trot and the pace are 2 forms of the same gait; in both gaits, 2 legs are used at once. If the 2 legs on one side are used together, it is called a pace. If diagonal legs are moved together, it is called a trot. The rhythm is the same, and the sound is the same.
(cited from: https://www.hiddentrails.com/article/horses_gaits.aspx)

In addition, there are several 4 beat "ambling" gaits. Any gait between walk and canter is considered an "intermediate" gait. A horse that performs an intermediate gait other than the trot is today called a "gaited" horse. In the early Americas and Europe at the time, this horse was known as an "ambler." The amble was the name given to a group of smooth, 4 beat gaits faster than a walk, but slower than a canter or gallop. An amble is achieved by the horse when it moves with a 4-step rhythm, either derived from the 2 beat lateral gait, known as the pace, or from the diagonal trot, with the 2 beats broken up, so there are 4. The trot is suitable for covering a lot of ground relatively quickly. However, in the trot, the horse also has a bit of a spring in its motion as it switches diagonal pairs of legs with each beat, and thus can be rough for a rider, and the trot also jostles about packs or weaponry to a considerable degree. The amble is about as fast as the trot, not tiring for a horse that performs it naturally, and much smoother for the rider. Thus, because much ground transportation in the Middle Ages was on horseback, with long distances to be covered, a smooth-gaited, ambling horse was very desirable.

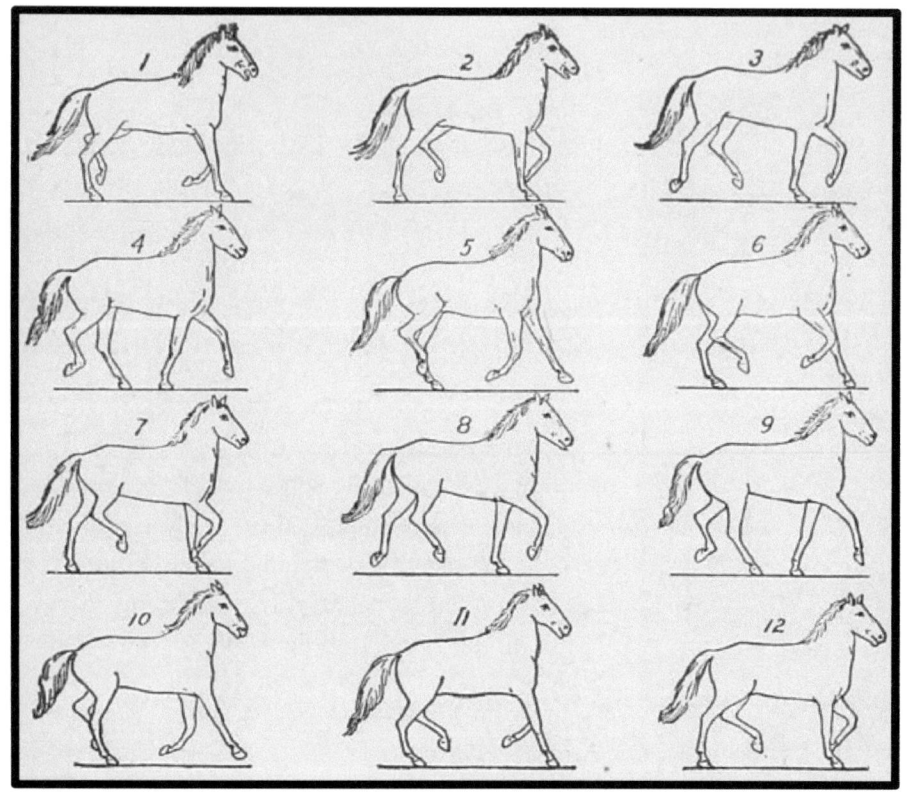

Ambling Horses (gaited)

The amble is a method of progressive motion with the same sequence of foot fallings as the walk, but in which a hind foot or a forefoot is lifted from the ground in advance of its fellow hind foot or its fellow fore foot being placed thereon. The support of the body, therefore, devolves alternately upon a single foot and upon two feet; the single foot being alternately a hind foot and a forefoot, and the two feet being alternately laterals and diagonals. At no time is the body entirely unsupported. The illustration *(left)* demonstrates the consecutive foot fallings and some characteristic phases of an ambling stride. *(cited from: Descriptive Zoopraxograph, 1893, by Eadweard Muybridge)*

Ambling horses are "gaited" horses. There are several 4-beat "ambling" gaits that are approximately the speed of a trot or pace, though smoother to ride. These include the lateral slow gait, rack, running walk, and tölt as well as the diagonal foxtrot. Ambling gaits are often genetic traits in specific breeds, known collectively as gaited horses. In most cases, gaited horses replace the standard trot with one of the ambling gaits. Ambling gaits are faster than the walk and often the trot but slower than the canter. Imports of Hobbies from Ireland along with English Running Horses were very popular in the Americas due to their speed and comfort. In the Americas, ambling horses were popular at first because there were few roads both in North America and in South America. Travel on uneven and rough terrain was much more comfortable when riding an ambling horse. Ambling gaits are smooth and can be sustained for long periods of time. Ambling horses were particularly desirable in the early America areas where plantation agriculture was practiced, and the inspection of fields and crops necessitated long daily rides. Ambling horses were also popular for transportation and post riders.

Running horses were very fast gaited horses. While they became extinct in England and Ireland, in America, these saddle horse traits have been kept alive; so much so that now gaited horses are found primarily only in the Americas. Genetic research in Ireland by Emmeline Hill and Mims Bower in 2010 and 2012 have discovered a "speed gene" in Thoroughbreds. The speed gene is a "sprint" gene; the speed of today's thoroughbreds originates from the early gaited horses!

In Colonial times if a horse was designated as a saddle horse that meant it was gaited and therefore comfortable.

Trotting Horses (walk, trot, canter, gallop)
Until posting was invented, the trotter was avoided as a saddle horse. Posting is to rise out of the saddle every other stride of the horse's forelegs, thus smoothing out the jolts encountered if just sitting. There are many stories about how/why posting was invented. One theory suggests that European royalty and aristocracy would opt to have a horseback rider driving the carriage/coach's team while mounted on one of the pulling horses as opposed to a low-life coachman riding up top with the rich folks. This is called postilion. *(left)* Eventually, these "post boys" discovered it was much easier to stand up in their stirrups with every other bounce of the horse as opposed to getting jostled around. As time went by, 'posting' became the accepted way to ride the trot. *(cited from: https://www.elkrivergr.com/blog/the-history-of-posting-the-trot-myths-debunked)*

Ambling horses eventually became uncommon in Europe. They were effectively replaced by trotting horses for several reasons; as roads improved, travel by carriage became more common and trotting horse breeds were generally larger and stronger. Trotting horses were primarily used for cavalry and harness work. Many ancient breeds (e.g., Arabian horses, Iberian horses) are trotters, but they have no speed at the trot. The speed at the trot comes from the infusion of pacing blood.

Classification of Use by Gait in the Early Americas
Saddle
    Amblers
Agriculture
    Walking Horses
Harness
    Trotting Horses
Racing
    Amblers
    Trotting Horses
Ranching
    Herding Horses (walk, trot, canter, fast sprint, agile)

The Purpose of Horses in the Early Americas

Early settlers to the Americas probably assumed the needs for horses would be the same as they had been in Europe – transportation, warfare, and farming. Little did they know that just surviving would be so difficult and that hippophagy (the eating of horse flesh) would be necessary for survival. As situations improved, more horses survived, and horses served many purposes. Until the last years of the 18th century, livestock received a significantly low amount of care. Domestic animals could survive only if they were strong enough to last through the winter, relying mainly on forests and natural meadowland for subsistence. Farmers became more attentive to the well-being of their animals when lucrative markets or sporting opportunities could be gained.

Hunting

Bounties to protect livestock were usually among the first edicts in the early colonies. In Plymouth, in 1624, a bounty of 2 pence was established per wolf "for the incouragement of persons to seeke the destruction of those ravenous creatures." This was changed to five bushels of corn in 1633, a more valuable commodity in the colony. Massachusetts Bay Colony Governor John Winthrop, writing in 1631, noted that the wolves "did much harm to calves and swine between Charles River and Mistic." The town enacted a bounty for wolves in November 1639. By 1641, it was law in Massachusetts for each man to "look daily after wolf traps." In Rhode Island, Roger Williams charged every townsman to rid the area of the "fierce, blood-sucking predators." Williams enlisted the aid of the Narragansett tribe to rid Aquidneck Island of its wolves, but the farms of Providence were still under siege. The town officially created a bounty in January 1659, when it was ordered that "whosoever shall from this tyme forward kill any woolves, that they shall have for each woolfe, a halfe penny a head for each head of catell ... provided they kill them within Providence Limetes." The bounties were of considerable profit to some. It was easier for a person on horseback to keep up with the hounds that were used for hunting the wolves, so horses were desirable for hunting. The wolf was the first animal hunted with hounds and horses in Virginia and Maryland.
(cited from: https://www.americanheritage.com/content/fox-hunting-america and http://www.providencejournal.com/opinion/commentary/20140207-robert-a.-geake-when-wolves-ranged-new-england.ece)

Farming

4 out of 5 colonists were farmers. Most colonists tilled fields using simple tools such as iron-bladed hoes. Plows were used by those wealthy enough to own horses. It was preferred that horses be at least 14 hands high, but most were smaller. They usually weighed between 600 and 700 pounds. *(cited from: http://www.history.org/Almanack/life/trades/traderural_horses.cfm)*

Transportation and Communication

Horses were the chief mode of transportation. When the colonies in the Northeast were first settled in the early 1600s, the communities lying between Boston and New York were virtually isolated from one another. On January 22, 1673, Governor Francis Lovelace of New York dispatched the first post rider *(left)* to effectively connect New York and Boston and provide mail service for the settlements which lay on the way. The route taken by this first post rider carried him to New Haven, Hartford, and then Springfield, Massachusetts. The route then followed the "Bay Path," a former Indian trail, on to Boston. This route was known as the Upper Boston Post Road, and the total journey from New York to Boston was some 250 miles. The post rider remained the principal means of communication in colonial America and his services were not replaced until improved roads permitted stagecoach travel in the late 1700s. The horse provided the means to carry goods to market, to speed people from one city to another, and to carry settlers into the interior of America. Muddy paths gave way to a well-designed road system. The stagecoach eventually afforded a means of mass transit whereby people could move about in relative safety and comfort *(cited from: http://www.imh.org/exhibits/online/legacy-of-the-horse/colonial-horses/)*

Commerce

Horses were a profitable commodity used for trade and export. The soil in New England was not well suited to farming, so horse breeding was seen as an economical use of hilly and infertile land. Back when Kentucky was only a remote and unknown woodland, the chief horse breeding region of America was Rhode Island. Rhode Island's horse industry got its beginning when John Hull, Treasurer of the Massachusetts Bay Colony, purchased land on the west side of Narragansett Bay from the local Indians. This area was fenced off and set up for horse breeding. At one time Rhode Island had farms with as many as 1,000 horses. These Rhode Island horses were shipped to all the sea-coast colonies as well as to the islands of the Caribbean for use on the plantations. *(cited from: http://www.imh.org/exhibits/online/legacy-of-the-horse/colonial-horses/)*

Ranching

After the Spanish arrived in Mexico in 1519, ranches were established and stocked with cattle and horses imported from Spain. When the first Spanish explorers came to the Americas, they brought cattle and cattle-raising expertise with them. Landowners mounted native Indians on well-trained horses and taught them to handle cattle. By the early 1700s, cattle ranching had spread north into what is now Texas, Arizona, and New Mexico and south to Argentina. A variety of ranching traditions developed in the Americas, depending on the region the settlers came from and the characteristics of the land where they settled. Gauchos are cowboys of the grasslands (or Pampas) of Argentina, Brazil, and Uruguay. In Central Mexico, particularly the state of Jalisco, cowboys are called charros *(left)*, like the charros from Castile, Spain, who settled the region. In Northern Mexico, wealthy ranchers known as Caballeros employed vaqueros to drive their cattle. Ranching in the western United States is derived from vaquero culture. *(cited from: https://www.americancowboy.com/ranch-life-archive/history-vaquero and) https://www.nationalgeographic.org/encyclopedia/ranching/)*

Conquests

Spanish horses were instrumental in the conquest of the New World. Neither the Aztec nor the Inca had ever seen humans riding animals before; the psychological impact of mounted troops was tremendous. Spanish conquistadors like de Soto were inheritors of some of the finest riding techniques in the whole of Eurasia. The jineta riding style, unique to Spanish cattle-ranchers, emphasized spontaneity, speed, balance in the saddle and maneuverability. *(cited from: http://www.pbs.org/gunsgermssteel/variables/horses.htm)*

This description of the Conquistadors and their horses is from an actual Aztec account:

"The 'stags' came forward, carrying soldiers on their backs. The soldiers wore cotton armor. They bore their leather shields and their iron spears in their hands, but their swords hung down from the necks of the stags. The animals wear many little bells. When they run, the bells make a loud clamor, ringing and reverberating. These animals snort and bellow. They sweat a great deal, and the sweat pours from their bodies in streams. Foam from their muzzles drips onto the ground in fat drops, like a lather of amole (soap). When they run, they make a loud noise, as if stones were raining on the earth. Then the earth is pitted and cracked open wherever their hooves have touched it." *(cited from: http://www.mexconnect.com/articles/682-the-aztecs-speak-an-aztec-account-of-the-conquest-of-mexico)*

Racing

The very first specially built race track in America was constructed in 1665 by New York's colonial governor Richard Nicholl. Called Newmarket *(left)* and located in the Hempstead Plains (just outside today's border with Queens), it proved an enduring enterprise for colonists. Smaller tracks were soon built in countryside closer to Manhattan island. Some aristocratic British landowners even built personal tracks on their estates. The track at Newmarket was "sixteen miles long and four wide, unmarred by stick or stone." *(cited from: http://www.boweryboyshistory.com/2011/05/why-go-to-Kentucky-new-yorks.html)*

Rhode Island had a one-mile track at Sandy Neck Beach, South Kingston. Many towns and cities in America have streets called "Race Street." Such streets gained their names from the habit of running horse races on them. In 1674, the citizens of Plymouth, Massachusetts evidently grew tired or frightened of the races in their villages and created an ordinance forbidding racing.

While horse racing generally followed English rules in the northern American colonies, another form of racing began to flourish in the southern regions. Quarter mile racing was a clear result of the geographical environment. The southeastern seaboard was mostly covered with dense forest. An immense effort was required to clear land, and it was therefore extremely valuable for agriculture. The racetracks in these wooded regions were sometimes little more than two parallel race paths, ¼ mile in length, cut through the forest. There was little space at either the beginning or the end of the track. The horses would sometimes be separated by a fence or trees. The quarter-mile track, therefore, gave both the race and the horses their name of "Quarter Horse." Horse racing was the principal form of organized sport in America. Modern towns have athletic rivalries on the football field. In colonial America, town rivalry was centered on horse racing. It was not unusual for the competitors and spectators to travel far to these early quarter-race tracks in the woods and to place considerable wagers on their town's horse. *(cited from: http://www.imh.org/exhibits/online/legacy-of-the-horse/colonial-horses/)*

In the Beginning……Breeding for the Purpose

In the early Americas horses existed to serve a purpose and breeding soon became less haphazard and more purposeful in order to achieve the needed purpose. Before breed registries, horses were organized by breeding practices and performance standards. Rhode Island became the breeding capital of the early North American Colonies. *(left: an ad from the* Providence Gazette and Country Journal, *January 7, 1764.)*

Size matters!

The first concern for the early settlers was size. In the early Americas, many of the horses brought from Europe were small. Settlers soon learned that a larger, more powerful and more versatile horse was needed. The Dutch horses were over 14 hands, and the English horses were under 13 hands. Stringent regulations were adopted against allowing under size colts and stallions to wander as they pleased. To foster quality in American horses, as early as 1668, the court of Massachusetts decreed that only horses "of comely proportions and 14 hands in stature" could graze on town commons. A law was enacted by William Penn in Pennsylvania in 1687 which set a minimum height of 13 hands for free-ranging horses. Any horse more than 18 months old and less than 13 hands had to be gelded. This really did not accomplish what was hoped. It was not until the close of the colonial days when farmers had facilities for breeding stock that there was an increase in the size of the horses. *(cited from: http://www.imh.org/exhibits/online/legacy-of-the-horse/colonial-horses/)*

Commerce

In less than 20 years after the New England colonies received their first supply of horses, they began to ship horses to Barbados and West India Islands to be used on the plantations. This continued into the 18th century. The pacers of the Rhode Island were highly desired; so much so that there were continuous raids by Spaniards on the Islands to steal the horses. This seems to indicate that had there been pacing horses among the horses of Spain, the Spanish dependencies would have secured their horses from Spain rather than steal them or go to Rhode Island and pay the high prices that the pacers brought.

Transportation

Travel was difficult due to the long distances between towns and the lack of roads. Again, the pacing/ambling horse was the answer. The pacing horses of Rhode Island were sought after for travel by many.

Ranching

The Irish Hobby Horse (the horse contributing to the ambling ability of early horses of the Americas) had a natural 'cow sense' and was used in Ireland to herd the cattle, the riders on horseback with whips would drive the cattle from one area to another. Couple that with the comfortable pacing gait, and again, the Rhode Island-bred horses were the desired horse for the job.

Racing

The horses brought to the colonies by the English were Irish Hobby horses; they were hardy and incredibly fast gaited horses. They were raced by colonists at all distances from a quarter mile up to 4 miles.

It did not take long for colonists to discover that racing was not only a way to impress others with one's status in life but also, a great form of entertainment for all! In

1624 selective breeding for quarter miles races was occurring in Jamestown, Virginia. In 1664 Governor Nicolls established a 2-mile course at Hempstead Plain on Long Island and the first race was held there in 1665. Governor Nicolls explained that the purpose of the race course was "not so much for the divertissement of youth as for encouraging the bettering of the breed of horses." To induce competition in the importing and careful breeding of horses, Nicolls offered trophies at the spring and fall meetings.

In the mid-1600's a one-mile track was built in Kingston, Rhode, Island. In northern Virginia, a racetrack was built in 1677 for races of 1 to 4 miles long. Racing in the colonies became very popular, and horse breeders bought and sold stock between the colonies, in order to improve the quality of the horses. By the 1700s many towns had race courses.

It was not until 100 years later, in 1730, that the first thoroughbred was imported to America from England.

Breeds of the Americas

Although there are many breeds of horses in the Americas, the breeds and types listed in this book are those that developed in the early Americas from the breeding of horses that were brought here by early explorers and settlers. DNA research has shed light on the origins of many breeds and research continues using this fairly new field of study. Some scientific and anthropological research has shown that what was thought about the origin of some breeds may not be entirely true. There are many unintentional inaccuracies arising from prevailing legends. Reviewing journals, writings and records from the various landings and early colonists, along with scientific research, helps to give us a better idea of the origins of the breeds of horses in the Americas.

Today, there are many breeds of horses in the Americas that are the result of cross-breeding the early breeds as well as crossbreeding many breeds and types of horses.

According to the Food and Agricultural Organization of the United Nations (FAO 2015), 87 horse breeds in the world are now extinct and among the remaining 905, almost a quarter are categorized as at risk.

Since its inception in 1977 (as the American Minor Breeds Conservancy, and later, the American Livestock Breeds Conservancy), The Livestock Conservancy has been a "central hub" for anything having to do with rare breed conservation in the United States. The Livestock Conservancy does research, education, outreach, marketing and promotion, and genetic rescues to help ensure the future of rare breed agriculture. Using this information, the Conservancy publishes America's list of endangered farm animal breeds and works to ensure those breeds aren't lost to extinction.

For each breed listed in this book, the status of the breed, if known, is listed in red after the name. The following categories are per the Livestock Conservancy.

Extinct: No longer exists

Critical: Fewer than 200 annual registrations in the United States and estimated global population less than 2,000.

Threatened: Fewer than 1,000 annual registrations in the United States and estimated global population less than 5,000.

Watch: Fewer than 2,500 annual registrations in the United States and an estimated global population less than 10,000. Also included are breeds that present genetic or numerical concerns or have a limited geographic distribution.

American Paint Horse (estimated population over 1,000,000 worldwide)
The origins of the Paint Horse in North America can be traced back to the two-toned horses introduced by the Spanish explorers. Inevitably, some of these colorful equines escaped creating the wild herds of horses roaming the Great Plains. Captured and gentled, they raced alongside the vast herds of buffalo and traveled hundreds of miles on cattle drives. Cherished by the finest horsemen of the Western frontier, both Native Americans and cowboys sought the hardy horses loudly splashed with color. Over time, breeders gradually improved the conformation and athletic ability of the rugged descendants of wild mustangs and cow ponies. Each generation passed its unusual and unique coat patterns and coloring to the next, creating the American Paint Horse.

Average Size: 14.2 to 16 hands, Body Type: Western Stock Horse, Colors: Combination of white with common horse colors, Coat Patterns: Tobiano, overo and tovero
(cited from: http://www.ansi.okstate.edu/breeds/horses/paint/index.html/)

Well Known Paint Horses and Owners
- Scout, Tonto's horse on the Lone Ranger *(above left)*
- Cochise, Little Joe's horse on Bonanza *(above right)*

American Quarter Horse (estimated population over 5,000,000 worldwide) The principal development of the Quarter Horse was in the southwestern part of the United States in Texas, Oklahoma, New Mexico, eastern Colorado, and Kansas. Some breed historians have maintained that it is the oldest breed of horses in the United States and that the true beginning of the Quarter Horse was in the Carolinas and Virginia. Nelson, C. Nye, in *Outstanding Modern Quarter Horse Sires*, has suggested that the Chickasaws secured from the Indians were the true beginning of the Quarter Horse. These were small blocky horses, probably of Spanish extraction, which the planters secured from the Indians, and which were adapted for a variety of uses. The colonists were quite interested in short races, and it was only natural that they should have attempted to increase the speed of their horses; to this end, some of the best early Thoroughbreds brought to the United States were instrumental in the improvement of these local running horses. In 1752, John Randolph of Virginia imported a grandson of The Godolphin Arabian, called Janus. When Janus was bred to Colonial mares bearing the blood of the Chickasaw horse, the result was the prototype of the American Quarter Horse. While it cannot be said that Janus founded the breed, it can be argued convincingly that he shaped and formed it significantly.

The early improvement in the Quarter Horse - so called because of its great speed at one-quarter of a mile - and the early development of the Thoroughbred in the United States was closely associated. Some sires contributed notably to both breeds. Many short-distance horses were registered in the American Stud Book as Thoroughbreds when the Stud Book was established, even though they did not trace in all lines to imported English stock.

It is more logical to assume that the true establishment of the Quarter Horse took place sometime later in the southwest range country rather than in colonial times. It was in the southwest that the true utility value of these short-distance horses was truly appreciated. The cowman found the Quarter Horse quick to start, easy to handle, and of a temperament suitable for handling cattle under a wide variety of conditions. Even in the Southwest much was unknown of the breeding of many of the horses that were classified and registered in the 1940s as Quarter Horses. It is logical, therefore, to conclude that until the Stud Book was established, and the pedigrees were based on fact rather than on memory and assumptions, the Quarter Horse should have been called a type of horse rather than a breed.

It is difficult to give the exact origin of the present-day Quarter Horse. Ranchers tried to breed the kind of horses on which men could work cattle, and that could also be used in the age-old sport of racing. The Quarter Horse was not raced on carefully prepared tracks but was raced on any suitable open space. Organized races were the exception rather than the rule with many of the races being run as a match race after a private wager between owner or riders. In the Southwest country as in the East, no particular attention was made to keep short-distance horses as a distinct breed. Fast horses whose offspring made good cow ponies were crossed on existing stock of mares. Many times, these mares carried Spanish, Arabian, Morgan, or Standardbred breeding. The naming of horses after persons was a common practice, and often when the horses were sold their names were changed; such practices have led to no end of confusion in attempting to verify pedigrees after the horses, breeders, and owners were deceased. *(cited from: http://www.ansi.okstate.edu/ breeds/horses/quarter/index.html)*

Modern American Quarter Horses are short and stocky, with heavy muscular development; short, wide heads; and deep, broad chests. They are fast starting, turning, and stopping ability and can maintain speed for short distances. Their colors are variable, but all are solid. The height of mature animals varies from 14.3 to 16 hands, and their weight varies from 950 to 1,200 pounds. They have a calm, cooperative temperament.

Well Known Quarter Horses and Owners
- Buttermilk - Dale Evans' horse *(above left)*
- George Strait owns Quater Horses *(above right)*
- Docs Keepin' Time portrayed Black Beauty in the 1994 film *(right)*

American Saddlebred (estimated population 75,000 worldwide)

After the American Revolution, the production of good Saddle Horses became a priority in Kentucky. These animals played a major role in the settlement of the upper Ohio Valley. They went south into Tennessee and beyond, and across the Mississippi into Missouri. Animals from Ohio, Indiana, Illinois, Iowa, and Tennessee all made contributions to the breed. Missouri rivaled Kentucky for the best Saddle Horses and Missourians say, "If Kentucky made the Saddle Horse, then Missouri made him better."

Horse shows became a popular form of public entertainment, often held at fairs. The first recorded show was in Lexington, Kentucky, in 1817, but such competitions undoubtedly took place years before. In 1856, St. Louis, the largest city west of the Mississippi, held its first great fair which featured the nation's first major horse show.

Denmark, the stallion who would be designated Foundation Sire of the breed, was foaled in 1839. By the time of the Mexican War in 1846, the American Saddlebred was a well-established breed. Entire companies of American volunteers from Kentucky and Missouri, mounted on these horses, fought in Mexico.

The American Saddle Horse gained fame as a breed during the Civil War. Since most Confederate horses were privately owned, General Grant's order at Lee's surrender, which allowed the men to keep their horses, perhaps saved the breed. The Confederate commands of Generals John Hunt Morgan and Nathan Bedford Forrest were mounted almost exclusively on American Saddlebreds, and these horses performed legendary feats of endurance during the war.

After the war, the St. Louis Fair was revived. All breeds had their day in competition at St. Louis, but in the 1870s the Denmarks became dominant. Because of the increased popularity and commercial value of the Saddlebred, enlightened breeders began to call for the formation of a breed association and registry in the 1880s. Charles F. Mills of Springfield, Illinois, began compiling pedigrees and formulating rules for a registry. The Farmers Home Journal, a newspaper published in Louisville, Kentucky, called for a meeting April 7, 1891, to organize the association and the registry was established that day; the first horse breed association in the United States. *(cited from: http://www.ansi.okstate.edu/breeds/horses/saddlebred/index.html)*

American Saddlebreds come in almost all colors, ranging in height from 14 to 17 hands and weigh 800-1,200 pounds.
The head and eye of the ideal American Saddlebred suggest refinement and intelligence. Long, sloping pasterns give a spring to the stride, making American Saddlebreds very comfortable to ride. High quality, smoothness, and balanced proportions complete an overall picture of symmetry and style.

Well Known Saddlebreds and Owners
William Shatner owns and shows Saddlebreds (below)
Traveller owned by Robert E. Lee (right)

Appaloosa (estimated population 500,000 worldwide)

The Appaloosa's heritage is as colorful and unique as its coat pattern. Usually noticed and recognized because of its spots and splashes of color, the abilities, and beauty of this breed are more than skin deep.

Humans have recognized and appreciated the spotted horse throughout history. Ancient cave drawings as far back as 20,000 years ago in what is now France depict spotted horses as do detailed images in Asian and 17th-century Chinese art.

The Spanish introduced horses to North America as they explored the American continents. Eventually, as these horses found their way into the lives of Indians and were traded to other tribes, their use spread until most of the Native American populations in the Northwest were mounted (about 1710).

The Nez Perce of Washington, Oregon, and Idaho became especially sophisticated horsemen, and their mounts, which included many spotted individuals, were prized and envied by other tribes. Historians believe they were the first tribe to breed selectively for specific traits - intelligence and speed - keeping the best and trading away those that were less desirable.

When white settlers came to the Northwest Palouse region, they called the spotted horses "Palouse horses." Over time the name was shortened and slurred to "Appalousey" and finally "Appaloosa."

During the Nez Perce War of the late 1800s, Appaloosa horses helped the Nez Perce avoid battles and elude the U.S. Cavalry for several months. The tribe fled over 1,300 miles of rugged, punishing terrain under the guidance of the famed Chief Joseph. When they were defeated in Montana, their surviving horses were surrendered to soldiers, left behind or dispersed to settlers. Nothing was done to preserve the Appaloosa until 1938 when a group of dedicated horsemen formed the Appaloosa Horse Club for the preservation and improvement of the diminishing spotted horse.
(cited from: http://www.ansi.okstate.edu/breeds/horses/appaloosa/index.html)

The base coat color may be any one of many colors and can include dilutes, duns, grays, roans and other modifying types. Eyes may be any color, including, but not limited to, blue, hazel, green, brown, amber and black. Coat color patterns may vary from a solid pattern, meaning no spotting at all, to multi-spotted to blanket hipped with no spots. Patterns and markings are extremely varied and found in many sizes and combinations with great variations in areas with white backgrounds. Appaloosas can dramatically change their coat pattern throughout their lifetime. No two Appaloosa horses are identically marked. *(from ApHC Standards guide)*

Well Known Appaloosas and Owners
- Zip Cochise, who was ridden by John Wayne in the 1966 movie "El Dorado" *(left)*
- 1936 Kentucky Derby winner Bold Adventure
- Assault (sired by Bold Adventure) who won the Triple Crown in 1946

5. This drawing of the stallion Louis XIV sent to Quebec in 1665 appears in the *Codex Canadiensis*. Either the animal was an Appaloosa or the artist was familiar with the "spotted horse" family from which the Appaloosa breed developed. *Courtesy of the Public Archives of Canada.*

Baguales

The Baguales *(left and below)* are a feral horse found in the Pampas region of Argentina. This is a tough, robust horse that is able to withstand highly variable climatic conditions. The Baguales breed originated in the 16th Century when Spanish stock was introduced to Argentina by conquistadors. Some animals escaped or were released to form feral herds that roamed the Pampas of the Rio de la Plata near Buenos Aires. Today, a few hundred Baguales horses remain within Torres del Paine Paine. However, the National Park authorities consider these horses as invasive and have ordered for their removal. Several research teams and non-profit organizations are working closely to prevent the possible extermination of these horses. The blood of this breed, along with that of horses from Brazil, Uruguay & Chile contributed to the blood of the Argentine Criollo. *(cited from: http://www.theequinest.com/breeds/baguales/)*

Banker Ponies (critical)

The Banker Ponies *(left and below)* inhabit the Outer Banks of the Carolinas and are also called Shackleford ponies, Banker Horses, and Ocracoke Ponies. They are believed to be descendants of Spanish horses brought by some first explorers to the area early in the 16th century. The Ocracoke ponies are thought to be descendants of a late 1500s shipwreck, the Tiger which explored the Eastern Seaboard under the direction of Sir Richard Greenville. After landing on Ocracoke, the horses had the island all to themselves for several centuries. The initial bloodlines of these animals were undoubtedly influenced by English horses as well as Spanish during early exploration. However, their blood has remained relatively pure due to their isolation. Features: Average height 13 – 14.3 hands, the head is simple with a broad forehead and generally convex profile, deep, narrow chest and short back, often lack chestnuts on hind legs. Traditional Colors: black | chestnut | bay | dun | pinto | buckskin. Temperament: Docile and friendly for feral ponies. Willing to learn and easy to train. *(cited from: http://www.theequinest.com/breeds/banker-pony/)*

Canadian Horse (critical)

The story of the Canadian Horse begins in 1665, when the French sun king, Louis XIV sent the first horses to New France to be distributed among the military officers of the Carignan-Salieres regiment. The first 14 royal horses destined for the New World left Le Havre on the ship Le Marie Therese on May 10, 1665. After 9 perilous and stormy weeks at sea, 2 stallions and 12 mares set hoof on the shores of New France at Tadoussac on July 16th. Another shipment of 15 royal horses arrived on September 25, 1667, with similar shipments reported in 1668, and 1669. In 1670, a stallion and 12 more mares arrived to be distributed among the gentlemen of New France. A final shipment of 13 horses arrived in 1671, for a total of 81 horses.

Northern French territory in those early times included not only Quebec but what is now Vermont, New York, Michigan, and Illinois. French horses found their way to the southern outposts, to French settlements at Chimney Point and Crown Point on the shores of Lake Champlain, and to the Jesuit missions near Detroit and on the shores of the Illinois River.

The horses adapted to their new frontier environment better than any other domestic animal sent to New France and soon became indispensable to the inhabitants: hauling wood, bringing in the harvest and maple sugar, working in the grinding mills, and providing much needed transportation over the ice of frozen rivers during the long cold winter months. The Canadian Horse became renowned for its abilities as a roadster, racer and stylish harness horse. By 1820, classes for Canadian Horses were being held at agricultural exhibitions in Lower Canada and in New York. Over the next decades, increasing numbers of Canadian horses, including the best stallions, were sold to the United States.

Had it not been for the tireless efforts of a small group of gentlemen inspired by patriotism, the Canadian Horse may well have disappeared from our landscape forever. Decades of depletion and crossbreeding had taken their toll, and the purpose of recording individuals not well understood by average horse-owners. In 1886, the first registry for 'La Race Chevaline Canadienne' was opened.

In the early 1900s the population of horses in Quebec dropped from 1 horse for every 5 inhabitants to 1 for less than every 10 inhabitants. *(above: born in 1913 Albert de Cap-Rouge became a very influential foundation sire.)*

By the end of 1940, Canada was heavily involved in World War II. Motor vehicles had largely replaced the horse in agriculture, transportation, and the military; once again, the alarm bell sounded for the fate of the Canadian Horse. In order to revive the breed, the association decided to temporarily re-open the stud-books in the early 1960s two mares that were of Canadian type but had no recorded ancestry. This second set of inspections continued throughout the critical period of the 1970s when breed numbers had dropped to less than 400, until 1984 when the stud books were again closed. Since then, all Canadian horses registered must come from 2 registered Canadian parents

In spite of dwindling to only a few hundred in the 1970s, and although still endangered, thanks to the efforts of dedicated breeders, owners, and admirers, the Canadian Horse is making a recovery. A genetic study conducted by researchers at the University of Guelph, Ontario in 2000, shows that the breed still maintains better genetic health than some other breeds with higher numbers, and is free from any known genetic defects.

Today's ideal Canadian Horse still closely resembles the spirited horse of over 150 years ago. A Canadian Horse typically stands 14 to 16 hands high, weighs 1000 to 1300 pounds, and is generally black with few, if any, white markings. Bays, chestnut, and occasionally rare champagne colors are found within the breed. The ideal Canadian has a finely chiseled head, strong arched neck, a long sloping shoulder, short back with well-muscled hindquarters, strong, flat-boned legs and exceptionally hard, strong hooves. The distinctive hallmark of the breed is its long, thick wavy mane and tail. The mane is often so thick that it falls on both sides of the neck and hangs below its shoulder, its tail so long that it touches the ground. Canadian Horses are confident, intelligent, hard-working, and sociable, and still, have all the endurance and adaptability of their ancestors.
(cited from: http://marielynnhammond.com /LegacyCanadians/2215103.htm)

Carolina Marsh Tacky (critical)

The Carolina Marsh Tacky or Marsh Tacky is a rare breed of horse, native to South Carolina. It is a member of the Colonial Spanish group of horse breeds, which also include the Florida Cracker Horse and the Banker horse of North Carolina. It is a small horse, well adapted for use in the lowland swamps of its native South Carolina. The Marsh Tacky developed from Spanish horses brought to the South Carolina coast by Spanish explorers, settlers and traders as early as the 16th century. The horses were used by the colonists during the American Revolution, and by South Carolinians for farm work, herding cattle and hunting. There are believed to be only 8 or 9 strains of Spanish colonial horses left in the US, and the Marsh Tacky is now documented as one of them. *(cited from: https://en.wikipedia.org/wiki/Carolina_Marsh_Tacky)*

Well Known Carolina Marsh Tacky Horses and Owners

- The US Coast Guard kept a small band of Banker ponies and Marsh Tackies to patrol the beaches in World War II. *(below)*

Chickasaw (extinct)

In the 18th century, 2 strains of Spanish horse were common along the Atlantic Seaboard – the Seminole or Creek horse originating in Florida (small and capricious in nature) and the Choctaw or Chickasaw horse (larger and more docile) originating in the plains west of the Mississippi River. (*above: Remington Park in Oklahoma became home to a beautiful Enoch Kelly Haney original statue, entitled "Chickasaw Horse and Rider"*). These types persist in Spanish Colonial horses of today. In 1784 these horses were described by J.F.D. Smyth in *A Tour of the United States of America* as "named from a nation of Indians who are very careful in preserving a fine breed of Spanish horses they have long possessed, unmixed with any other." This stock was widely distributed and bred along the Atlantic Seaboard throughout the 18th century. In time, a wide variety of Indian horses were termed "Chickasaws." It was not necessarily a breed but a type of desirable saddle horse. They were described in 1809 by David Ramsay, a prominent historian, as "handsome, active and hardy but small; seldom exceeding 13 hands and a half in height. The mares in particular, when crossed with English blooded horses, produced colts of great beauty, strength, and swiftness." *(cited from: The Wild Horse Dilemma)*

Chilean Horse
The Chilean horse *(left and below)* is the oldest registered American stock horse breed of Iberian origin. It was started in about 1544 by Father Rodrigo Gonzalez Marmolejo in New Toledo. It has the reputation of being the best horse in South America but is virtually unheard of outside of South America. As a former warhorse, the popularity of Chilean Rodeo has kept the breed alive.

Chincoteague Ponies (threatened)

Two herds of wild horses make their home on Assateague Island, separated by a fence at the Maryland-Virginia line. These small but sturdy, shaggy horses have adapted to their environment over the years by eating dune and marsh grasses and drinking fresh water from ponds. While they appear tame, they are feral, and Park Rangers urge visitors not to feed or pet them. The Maryland herd is managed by the National Park Service. The Virginia herd is owned by the Chincoteague Volunteer Fire Company. Each year the Chincoteague Volunteer Fire Company purchases a grazing permit from the National Fish and Wildlife Service. This permit allows the Fire Company to maintain a herd of approximately 150 adult ponies on Assateague Island. The Fire Company controls the herd size with a pony auction on the last Thursday in July. Each year tens of thousands of spectators come to watch the Saltwater Cowboys swim the pony herd from Assateague Island to Chincoteague Island. *(above)*.

A book was written by Mr. John Amrhein, "The Hidden Galleon," describes the wreck of a Spanish galleon, the La Galga, in 1750. Its location, the circumstances of the voyage, the great storm of 1749, which decimated all the livestock on Assateague Island prior to the La Galga wreck, and the appearance of "Beach" Ponies shortly after the demise of the La Galga, and other evidence strongly suggest this to be the origin of the ponies. While not absolute the circumstantial evidence he presents is very powerful. For more information go to www.thehiddengalleon.com. *(cited from: http://www.chincoteague.com/ponies.html)*

Well Known Chincoteague Ponies and Owners

In 1947, Marguerite Henry *(left with Misty)* published *Misty of Chincoteague*, the story that made Pony Penning internationally famous. A movie followed, as did several sequel books. The tale of the wild pony Phantom, her foal Misty and the children who buy and raise her have become a classic, still loved and enjoyed by each new generation.

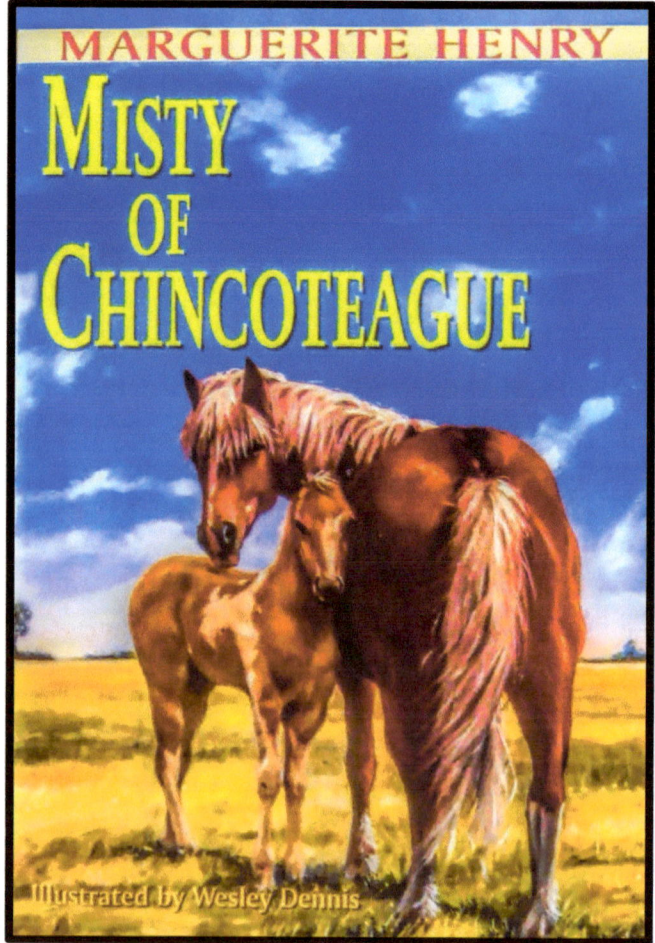

Colonial Spanish Horses (threatened)
Strains:
 Baca-Chica
 Choctaw
 Santa Cruz
 Sulfur
 Wilbur-Cruce (111 known)

As the Narragansett Pacer faded into obscurity, the Spanish horse moved into the limelight. According to D. Phillip Sponenberg, DVM, Ph.D., a professor at Virginia-Maryland Regional College of Veterinary Medicine, the earliest Spanish horses imported to North America, including the populations of the southeastern United States, were typically brought from Mexico. After these original introductions, it was uncommon for planters to import horses directly from Spain into these local populations. In South America however, the earliest horses came from the Antilles, followed by repeated importations of horses form the Caribbean and Spain. This divergence in bloodlines gave rise to the numerous distinct types of pure Colonial Spanish Horses of today. Around 1700 the purely Spanish horse was found in an arch that stretched northward from Florida, through the Carolinas, Tennessee and the Great Plains and into the western mountains. These horses averaged under 13.2 hands, and many were gaited. By the mid-1700's great numbers of untended Spanish horses roamed the Southeast. The Colonial Spanish horse of today is 13 to 15 hands; 750 to 1,000 pounds and reaches full maturity at 7 to 9 years. Gaits will be smooth and comfortable whether lateral or diagonal. Many colors including bay, black, blue corn, brown, buckskin, chestnut, dun, gray, grullo, ysabella, palomino, roan, and white. Color patterns include Appaloosa, tobiano, overo, Medicine Hat, War Bonnet, calico, sabino, frame and splash paint plus many variations. There are three distinct types and other intermediate types which fall somewhere between these three:

The lighter bodied and leggy horse is called the light or SOUTHWESTERN type.

The heavy or Northern type is a blockier horse like the SPANISH JENNETT.

The third resembles the ANDALUSIAN, the classic Spanish horse seen in Renaissance art.

(cited from: The Wild Horse Dilemma and http://horseoftheamericas.com/conformation.html)

Conestoga Horse (extinct)

CONESTOGA

The Conestoga Horse *(left)* was developed in the United States during the 18th and early 19th centuries for pulling the famous Conestoga wagons that were produced in Lancaster County, Pennsylvania. The Conestoga Valley was settled in the early 18th century. It was then wilderness but a country of unsurpassed fertility. Its first homemakers were farmers. They came from the upper Rhine country and Switzerland. With them came a good number of French Huguenots. These people needed horses for many things, all of which were hard work. These horses were not bred by any scientific system but by process of natural selection. As generation succeeded generation a horse evolved that met the demands placed upon it by understanding owner

Benjamin Rush, writing in 1789 states, "A large, strong wagon covered with a linen cloth is an essential part of a German farm. In this wagon, drawn by 4 or 5 horses, a peculiar breed, they convey to market over the roughest roads, 2,000 to 3,000 pounds of produce from their farms." Undoubtedly the horses "of a peculiar breed" which attracted the attention of Dr. Rush, were Conestogas. According to the late Dr. Herbert Beck of Lancaster, who was an authority on horses, the first authentic record which he found on Conestoga horses under that name, appears in *"The Cabinet of Natural History and American Rural Sports,"* published in 1832. Under the heading "The American Horse," 3 breeds are listed. These are the Canadian, the English, and the Conestoga. Of the latter the writer states, "The Conestoga horse is found in Pennsylvania, long in limb and light in the carcass, sometimes rising to 17 hands." Dr. Beck maintained that it was the only kind of horse bred for that purpose in the United States.

As settlers began heading west from Pennsylvania, more and more horses were needed to pull their heavy wagons. The Conestoga wagon was designed to meet this need, and the Conestoga horse was called upon to power it. In hauling these wagons over the Allegheny Mountains, the Conestoga won its place in the story of American transportation. *(cited from: http://articles.mcall.com/1988-03-06/entertainment/2614046_1_five-horses-conestoga-breed)*

Well Known Conestoga Horses and Owners
- It is thought that horses owned by Samuel Gist (the man who imported the first Thoroughbred to America) and George Washington may have been used for breeding in the development of Conestoga horses.

Criollo

The Criollo horse *(left: Gloria Austin Driving Four Criollo Horses This windy day in Argentina blew Gloria's hat away.)* is the direct descendant of the horses brought to the Americas by the Spanish. When the Spanish horse was left free in this new habitat, it had to adapt itself to the new conditions, protect itself against the threatening dangers and carry on reproduction under the law of survival of the aptest. In short, the Criollo horse is the product of 4 centuries of life in the open air, of an adaptation to the environment and of strict natural selection.

Throughout the 19th century, a large proportion of the horses were crossed with imported European Thoroughbred, coach and draft horse stallions, and a larger, coarser, long-striding multi-purpose, saddle cart horse resulted. However, the crossbreeding nearly ruined the native Spanish horse type. In Uruguay, the Genealogical Registers were opened in 1929, and in 1941 the Uruguayan Criollo Horse Breeder's Society was founded with the fundamental objective of caring for the purity of the breed. The breeders implemented rigorous endurance tests to help evaluate horses for breeding. In these events known as "La Marcha," the horses are ridden over a 466-mile course to be completed in 75 hours split in 14 days. No supplemental feed is allowed. The horses are required to carry heavy loads of 245 pounds on their backs and may only eat the grass at the side of the road. At the end of the day, a veterinarian checks the horses. The Criollo is a medium sized horse (13 – 14 hands). It is mainly used for farm work but is also used as a draft horse and for pleasure riding. Predominant colors are chestnuts, dun, Auburn, roan, and tobiano layers. Features are the dark stripe along the spine, also known as 'mule stripe,' and the cebraduras or zebra stripes on the legs, also known in Ecuador as mishimaqui or cat hand *(cited from: http://afs.okstate.edu/breeds/horses/criollouruguay/index.html and https://en.wikipedia.org/wiki/Criollo_horse and https://www.criollo-horse.com/en/history-of-the-criollo-breed.html)*

Florida Cracker Horse (critical)

The genetics of the Florida Cracker breed comes from the Iberian horse of the early 16th century Spain and includes blood from the North African Barb, Spanish Sorraia, and the Spanish Jennet. These horses also contributed to the Spanish Mustang, Paso Fino, Peruvian Paso, and Criolla breeds, so the Florida Cracker's genetic base is very similar to theirs.

These horses were used by Florida cowmen, termed "Crackers" from the sound of cow whips cracking, and the name stuck to the horses as well. However, in the 1930s, the Great Depression affected the Florida Cracker breed as severely as it affected most things. Many cattle needed to be transported into Florida to escape the Dust Bowl, but they brought with them the screwworm fly. This new parasite created new challenges in cattle management, and the cattle now required new fencing and dipping vats. The Florida Cracker horse was too small and too weak to meet the cowmen's new needs, and instead, they turned to the Quarter Horse to rope and hold cattle for the screwworm treatment. Demand for the Florida Cracker Horse fell, and they became a rarity.

A few families continued the breed, raising them for their own ranches and kept the breed from extinction. In 1989, the Florida Cracker Horse Association was formed to search for the remaining Florida Cracker horses. In May 2008, Florida lawmakers voted the Florida Cracker Horse Florida's official horse.

These horses are small, saddle suited, at 13.2 to 15.2 hands and weigh 700-1000 lbs. They can be any color, although solid colors, namely gray, are most prevalent. Their gaits cover ground well, including the flat-footed walk, running walk, trot, and ambling gait; these are possible with no special shoeing, and often, even barefooted. They do not share the crested appearance of the neck associated with some Spanish breeds, instead of being fairly narrow and having the same length as the withers-to-croup distance. *(cited from: http://afs.okstate.edu/breeds/horses/florida-cracker-horse)*

Galiceño (critical)

The Galiceños are small horses, 12 to 13.2 hands high, extraordinarily strong, agile, and possess tremendous stamina. These horses are narrow in the chest and have a short back (like Arabians). They are nicely proportioned with fine features, small alert ears, and a narrow but straight or convex snout. Their color includes black, bay, browns, sorrel (chestnut), buckskin, palomino, gray and roans. There are no Appaloosa or Paints in the breed. They are very intelligent, quick to learn and eager to please. Most are gaited with an extended running walk. Their movement is generally smooth. They have an excellent disposition, friendly and curious.

Although Galiceños are of pure Iberian heritage, they are a "landrace" distinguished from other Colonial Spanish Horse breeds and strains by their small size and gait.

Preliminary results of genetic tests done by Dr. E. Gus Cothran at Texas A&M University on Galiceños show them to be closest to the Garrano horses of Portugal, a primitive horse of the Iberian Peninsula. When Columbus returned to the "New World" on his second voyage, he brought small horses and established breeding herds on Hispaniola and Cuba. All subsequent voyages from Spain brought more Iberian horses to the Islands. Hernan Cortes followed in the early 1500s also bringing horses to Cuba from the Iberian Peninsula. In 1519 when he invaded the mainland of Mexico, establishing a stronghold near Veracruz, he brought along some of these horses which significantly impressed the natives and resulted in them believing the Spaniards were "gods" thereby making it easier for the Spaniards to conquer the native peoples. Reinforcements brought more horses to the mainland for the Spaniards who were taking over Mexico. Later, even more, horses were brought to the mainland with the settlers, colonists, and missionaries as they settled Mexico. There, some of those horses bred, and through natural selection rather than the artificial selection of humans, resulted in the horses now called "Galiceños." They are considered a distinct "landrace" *(a domesticated, locally adapted, traditional variety of a species of animal or plant that has developed over time, through adaptation to its natural and cultural environment of agriculture and pastoralism, and due to isolation from other populations of the species)* descended from the earliest "Colonial Spanish Horses" in the Americas and are very pure Spanish horses in the sense that there has been little if any genetic exchange with other breeds because of their isolation. Many of these horses were brought into the United States from 1958 through the mid-'60's to establish the US registry of the Galiceño Horse Breed. *(cited from: http://www.galiceno.org/index.html)*

Mangalarga Marchador (350,000+ registered)

The most popular and widespread horse in Brazil is the Mangalarga Marchador, which developed in 1740. Joao Francisco of Portugal settled in Brazil at the Hacienda Campo Alegre, where the Marchador horses began to emerge. Francisco adopted the surname Junqueira to designate his native city. One of his 12 children, Gabriel Francisco Junqueira, the Baron of Alfenas, is credited with the expansion and development of the breed. His friend, Dom Pedro I (1798-1834), Emperor of Brazil and son of Joao IV of Portugal, gave him an Alter Real stallion named Sublime. The stallion Sublime was the descendant of 2 horses brought from the breeding farm Coudelaria Alter do Chao in Portugal by Dom Joao VI during the invasion of the Iberian Peninsula by Napoleonic troops. In Brazil, Sublime was crossed with mares of the Hacienda Campo Alegre: Spanish Jennets and Andalusians. Most of the Spanish horses used at the hacienda in launching the breed were the famous Spanish Jennet, known to be a fast, smooth ambler. The offspring of Sublime produced horses with the characteristics of the present-day Mangalarga Marchador horse. The Mangalarga Marchador has, as the true expression of the breed, the "Marcha." This is an accelerated gait that maintains regularity making the ride very smooth and comfortable for the rider. During the "marcha," the Mangalarga Marchador makes a semicircle with the anterior legs and uses the posterior legs as leverage, thus propelling the animal forward. When in movement the Mangalarga Marchador executes an alternation of diagonal and lateral supports, always softened by an intermediate time: the triple support. This is the movement when three of the horse's hooves touch the ground at the same time.

It is a light horse but strong and well-muscled. The front is light with a triangular head and a pyramidal neck. The body is strong with well-arched ribs. The legs show vigorous and well-formed tendons. It is a horse of medium stature, measuring, 14.2 to 16 hands. Although grays predominate, chestnut, black, bay, buckskin, palomino and paint horses are also present. The sturdiness of this breed can easily be noted as one observes its great adaptability to any type of adverse terrain or climate, be it tropical, temperate or cold. Its endurance is demonstrated by its capacity for traveling long distances without fatigue. The Mangalarga Marchador is not a demanding feeder, surviving well on a regime of either partial stabling or open field which, for the owner means low cost and freedom from the usual problems caused by the diversity of pasture. It is also quite resistant to disease and parasites.

As with many Iberian breeds, they are good cattle horses. They are known for setting the Guinness Book of World Records endurance ride of 8,694 miles in 1994. A perfect trail horse, they excel in other disciplines that require agility, stamina, speed, and a sound mind. *(cited from: http://afs.okstate.edu/breeds/horses/mangalarga/index.html and http://www.namarchador.org/breed/)*

Missouri Fox Trotter (42,283 registered)

Missouri achieved statehood in 1821, and the pioneers who poured across the Mississippi River and settled in the Ozarks came largely from Tennessee, Kentucky, and Virginia. Naturally, they brought along their saddle horses, descendants of the early colonial ambling horses, popular in those areas. It soon became apparent that horses able to perform the easy, broken gait called the Fox Trot were the most useful in the rocky, forest-covered hills of the Ozarks and selective breeding for the Fox Trot gait began. Easy gaited stock imported to our nation's shores during the Colonial era left their genetic imprint on the Fox Trotting Horses of the Ozarks, the American Saddle Horses of Kentucky, and the Walking Horses of Tennessee.

The distinguished characteristic of the Missouri Fox Trotting Horse is the Fox Trot gait; the horse walks with the front feet and trots with the hind feet. This extremely sure-footed gait gives the rider little jar since the hind feet slide into place. The Fox Trot is a rhythm gait, and the horse can maintain it for long periods of time with little fatigue. The Missouri Fox Trotter also performs a rapid flat foot walk and a delightful canter.

Fox Trotters became the using horse of the Ozarks. They were the favorite mounts of cattlemen, country doctors, sheriffs, and tax assessors before improved roads and cars appeared on the scene. Missouri ranks number two in the nation in cow-calf operations, and Missouri Fox Trotting Horses are historically tied to the grazing cattle industry of the Ozarks. When automobiles made horses almost obsolete in the everyday lives of most Ozarkians, Missouri Fox Trotting Horses survived largely because the cattlemen of the region continued to use and breed them.

Stamina, soundness, and gentle disposition were serious considerations in the breeding of Fox Trotting Horses by pioneer families in the Ozarks. They range from 14 to 16 hands, colors are: Black, roan, champagne, brown, cremello, grullo, dun, palomino, buckskin, perlino, coupled with white markings on the face and leg They have a straight face profile, muscular body, medium-length neck ending in withers, well-shaped pointed ears, bright eyes, tapered muzzle, sloped shoulders, short back and sturdy legs, well-proportioned and properly shaped hooves. Missouri Fox Trotters are Docile, calm, reliable, placid, good-natured disposition, loves human company. *(cited from: http://afs.okstate.edu/breeds/horses/missourifoxtrotting/index.html)*

Well Known Missouri Fox Trotters and Owners

Missouri Fox Trotters are popular horses for forest rangers due to their comfort, secure footing and reliability on the trails

Willie Hedgpeth of Nixa stands on the back of the great Fox Trotter stud out of Old Fox, Ozark Golden King.

Morgan (80,000 registered)

The Morgan Horse is an America Legend. The breed was the official horse of the American Bicentennial.

The horse known as Justin Morgan's horse started life as a small, rough-coated colt known as "Figure." *(left)* He was born in 1789, and in 1791, he left his birthplace in Springfield, Massachusetts with his new owner, the soft-spoken schoolteacher Justin Morgan, by whose name the stallion eventually became known. Although his breeding was unknown (thought to be of Dutch, Thoroughbred, or Arabian breeding), the quality of Justin Morgan's ancestry showed in his straight clean legs; deep muscling over his quarters and shoulders; and fine, intelligent head with large expressive eyes and short, pricked ears. Add to these the quality of his movement, a thick but silky mane and tail, and a clean-cut throatlatch, and you have the conformation of the ideal light horse. Despite these fine qualities, Justin Morgan's lack of size was such that his debt-ridden owner found no buyers on their journey north to Randolph Center, Vermont. It was simply fated that no one but, his new owner realized what a little giant he was.

Over the next 30 years, the little bay stallion worked long, hard hours in the fields and on the roads of Vermont. Gradually, the local population began to talk about the feats of "the Justin Morgan horse." Standing just over 14 hands tall, Justin Morgan's exploits gained him fame because he was not as big as colonial workhorses nor as tall and long-legged as racehorses, yet he consistently outperformed both. There was the time he pulled a log no draft horse could budge, the day only he had the beauty, spirit, and manners to carry President James Monroe on a muster-day parade ground; and the time he outran the most winning racehorse central Vermont had ever known, at least until that day.

Doing it all and doing it well, Justin Morgan remained sound of eye, wind, and limb throughout a lifetime of two ordinary horses. That should have been enough, but the stallion added still more: showy, ground-covering gaits with speed to spare at any one of them; a gentle disposition that made him safe enough for a child to handle yet spirited enough for any horseman, beauty men would recall decades after his death; and a rare courage that made men who lost bets on him hit their flagons of rum and say, 'To the little Morgan!' and drink deeply.

Justin Morgan also proved to be one of the greatest breeding horses of all time. As the saga of the little stallion grew, countless mares were bred to him. So prepotent were the genes of this stallion that no matter what type of mare he was bred to, be the mare of the heavy draft or refined racing-type, his offspring inherited his image and abilities. While most breeds develop by breeding horses of similar characteristics to each other, Justin Morgan's ability to pass his characteristics to his offspring for generations to come allowed this single stallion to found an entire breed in his likeness. Today, every registered Morgan traces back to Justin Morgan through his best-known sons Bulrush, Sherman, and Woodbury.

In the coming years, the offspring of these strong, willing, able light horses grew along with the young nation that was building itself upon hard work and determination. In the hands of American colonists, Morgans cleared rugged Vermont mountainsides and converted them into rich farmland. But they weren't mere workhorses, Morgans had the style and elegance to capture the admiration of any city horseman. While some Morgans earned their keep on the farm others were in high demand to become smart roadsters for Boston and New York financiers. When harness racing reached its heyday in the 1800s, the World's Fastest Trotting Stallion was Ethan Allen 50, old Justin's handsome great-grandson.

As America grew so did the feats of the Morgan. New England men answered the call of gold and headed for California on Morgans. In the Civil War, the famed Vermont Cavalry was mounted on Morgan horses. Not only did the Union's General Sheridan ride his Morgan Rienzi, *(left)* Stonewall Jackson rode his Morgan, 'Little Sorrel,' for the Confederacy as well!

In the Indian Wars, the only survivor in the Battle of the Little Big Horn was Keogh's Morgan-bred horse Comanche. If the pathways of history are paved with the bones of the horse, surely America's are paved by Morgans.

While the offspring of Justin Morgan was taming the wilderness and building the country, they were also creating the standards by which other American breeds would become known. The stamina and vigor of the Morgan together with his excellent conformation and way of going helped make other American light horse breeds what they are today. The great speed of today's racing Standardbreds was produced by crosses to the fastest Morgan blood. In the 1860s, the Morgan stallion Shepherd F. Knapp was exported to England where his trotting speed became a byword. Today, many English Hackneys carry his name in their pedigrees. In American Saddlebreds, such famous champions as Edna May, Bourbon King, Rex Peavine, and Wing Commander trace to Justin Morgan. The foundation sire of the Tennessee Walking horse, Allen F-1, was a grandson of the Morgan stallion Bradford's Telegraph. In addition, many good Morgan mares were sent to Texas only to lose their breed identity in Quarter Horse bands, and to make the breed greater for it. The oldest of all-American breeds the Morgan was strong enough to contribute greatly to almost every other American light horse breed while retaining its own identity across two centuries.

Present-day Morgans differ little from their mighty progenitor. (*left: UVM Flash in front of the statue of Justin Morgan (Figure) in Vermont, believed to be in the 1970s, to show conformation consistencies with the original Morgan*) The average size of a Morgan today is between 14.2-15.2 hands, with some individuals over or under. Morgan coats are predominantly chestnut, bay, or brown, although many black, palomino, buckskin, and even a few grays appear in the breed. The breed's tremendous courage, disposition, substance, and type has remained as important to breeders today as it was 200 years ago. Whether you visit farms in New England, California, or any state in between, you can see bands of Morgans with the same deep bodies, lovely heads, and straight clean-boned legs. In barns and show rings across the country, the Morgan show horses flash by with heads high, eyes bright, and nostrils wide - Morgan quality showing in every hair on their gleaming, muscular bodies.

Today, Morgans have few wildernesses to conquer or wars to win, but they still accomplish great deeds. They are loved and revered as dynamite performers in Morgan shows across the country, and as loyal, sensible mounts on America's beautiful trails and pathways; they are treasured by mounted police squads and therapeutic riding programs for their intelligence, soundness, and gentleness; they are winning awards in driving, dressage, reining and cutting competitions against horses bred specifically for these jobs; and no matter what they may be doing or the tack they wear, knowledgeable horsemen see them and know, 'That's a Morgan!'

A bit of the hard-working determined Morgan legend is with us whenever a Morgan carries a saddle-weary cowhand down a Montana mountain, pulls a carriage around a grueling obstacle course in record time, quietly carries children along a wooded path, or flashes around show rings with a style that causes spectators to cheer. The Morgan, our country's first breed of light horse, is as much a part of America today as it was two centuries ago.'

The Morgan legend has also spread around the world. Morgan owners and dubs can be found in Canada, England, Germany, Italy, France, Australia, New Zealand, Mexico, and South America. The beauty, intelligence, and willing personality of the Morgan will win you over too! *(cited from: http://afs.okstate.edu/breeds/horses/morgan/index.html)*

Well Known Morgan Horses and Owners
Many famous officers rode Morgens during the Civil War, and the following regiments of the cavalry were mounted on Morgans at the beginning of the war: First Maine Cavalry, Second Michigan Cavalry, Third Michigan Cavalry, Fourteenth Pennsylvania Cavalry, Fifth New York Cavalry Company H

Marguerite Henry's popular book, "Justin Morgan Had a Horse" was also made into a movie by Disney *(left)*

Mustang (approximately 67,000 roaming on public lands in 10 Western states)

The Mustang is a free-roaming horse of the American West. The name was derived from the Spanish word mustengo, which means "ownerless beast" or "stray horse." The original Mustangs were Colonial Spanish horses, but many other breeds and types of horses contributed to the modern Mustang, resulting in varying phenotypes. Since Mustangs are descendants of escaped domesticated horses, wildlife management agencies consider them to be "feral" rather than "wild," although this designation is controversial among mustang advocates. The Bureau of Land Management (BLM) is tasked to uphold the 1971 legislation "The Wild Free-Roaming Horses and Burros Act," written to protect these free-roaming horses. The issue is complex and has many conflicting interests, from those who want to see the horses stay free, to those who object to the strategies used for limiting herd growth, to ranchers who graze their livestock on public land and view the Mustangs as competition. These horses and burros can be found mainly on government-designated Herd Management Areas (HMA) in 10 western states: Arizona, California, Colorado, Idaho, Montana, Nevada, New Mexico, Oregon, Utah, and Wyoming. The Mustang is not on any endangered list at this time, though there are people petitioning to change that. About 100 years ago, about 2,000,000 mustangs roamed the North American terrain, and now there are approximately 67,000. Mustangs are a medium-sized breed of horse. They measure around 14 to 15 hands. Mustangs have a wide variety of colors. They can also have a variety of patches, spots, and stripes. They are a hardy horse; often living to 40 years old. *(cited from: https://www.mnn.com/earth-matters/animals/stories/mustangs-of-the-west-why-this-american-icon-is-disappearing and https://www.livescience.com/27686-mustangs.html)*

Photo by Jeanne Bencich Nations

Narragansett Pacer (extinct)

The Narragansett Pacer *(etching from Frank Forester's Horse and Horsemanship of the United States and British Provinces of North America 1857)* made valuable contributions too many breeds of North America. The horse is named for the area from which they developed – the Narragansett Bay area of Rhode Island. Their ancestors were probably among the English and Dutch horses which arrived in Massachusetts between 1629 and 1635. The Dutch horses were 14 hands or over, and the English horses were nearer to 13 hands; most likely Irish Hobby horses. The Narragansett Pacer was known as a saddle horse that provided a comfortable ambling gait that was sure-footed; they had great endurance.

Most races in the early colonies were with gaited horses. The Narragansett Pacer was swift indeed! He could pace a mile in just over 2 minutes. Not only were they great horses for racing - a pastime that was very popular – but they also made great saddle horses. Transportation at the time was on rough roads, and the easy ambling gait of the Narragansett Pacer made them incredibly desirable.

The Narragansett Pacer was the primary export and chief source of income for the area. It was bred in vast numbers in the 1700s and exported to plantations in Cuba and the Islands. The breed reigned as the most desirable saddle horse for a century and a half.

The breed eventually became extinct as colonial roads improved and people began to drive trotting horses more than ride these ambling, smooth gaited horses.

The horses were diminutive; 13 – 14 hands. Despite efforts to increase their size, this never happened due to the system prevalent everywhere of horses roaming at large. The best description of these unusual pacing horses is given by Robert Livingston in an article on American agriculture in the first American edition of the Edinburgh Encyclopedia written about 1830. The description reads as follows:

"They have handsome foreheads, the head clean, the neck long, the arms and legs thin and taper; the hindquarters are narrow and the hocks a little crooked, which is here called sickle hocked, which turns the hind feet out a little: their color is generally, though not always, bright sorrel; they are very spirited and carry both head and tail high. But what is most remarkable is that they amble with more speed than most horses trot so that it is difficult to put some of them upon a gallop. Notwithstanding this facility of ambling, where the ground requires it, as when the roads are rough and stony, they have a fine, easy single-footed trot. These circumstances, together with their being very sure-footed, render them the finest saddle horses in the world; they neither fatigue themselves nor their rider. It is generally to be lamented that this invaluable breed of horses is now almost lost by being mixed with those imported from England and from other parts of the United States."

The sturdy qualities of the Narragansett pacers have also been perpetuated by James Fenimore Cooper in his tales of the American wilderness. He seats his heroine, Alice Munro, on a Narragansett Pacer in *The Last of the Mohicans*. The horses were evidently still obtainable in Cooper's day, and he must have been an admirer of the breed, for he brings them into his stories frequently.

(cited from: https://archive.org/stream/horseraisinginco00phil/horseraisinginco00phil_djvu.txt)

The British politician Edmund Burke wrote an *Account of the European Settlements in America* in 1857 that noted the emerging breeds of horses in New England: "They have, besides, a breed of small horses which are extremely hardy. They pace naturally though in no very graceful or easy manner; but with such swiftness, and for so long a continuance, as must appear almost incredible to those who have not experienced it." *(cited from: http://www.newenglandhistoricalsociety.com/narragansett-pacer-lost-horse-new-england-colonies/)*

Well Known Narragansett Pacers and Owners
- George Washington owned a pair of Narragansett Pacers, which he highly valued. He wrote about racing them in his diary.
- Esther Forbes, Paul Revere's Pulitzer Prize-winning biographer, argues forcibly that the horse that Revere rode from Charlestown to Lexington was a Narragansett Pacer, but this has been debated. *(above left)*

Newfoundland Pony (critical)

The Newfoundland's history is an excellent example of what it takes to make a breed. Like many breeds, its roots are in several older breeds that came to the Newfoundland province of Canada with colonists in the 17th and 18th centuries. Early settlers brought from the British Isles Exmoor, Dartmoor, New Forest, Galloway, Welsh, Connemara, and the odd Highlands ponies. These ponies, for nearly 3 centuries, interbred until one common pony developed, "The Newfoundland Pony." DNA studies published in 2011 confirmed the unique genetic makeup of this breed

In their new home, the fledgling breed was isolated from its foundation stock and was strongly influenced by the maritime environment and its use by local farmers and fishermen in plowing, hauling, and transporting goods and people. These hardworking and loyal ponies hauled firewood, timber, kelp, rocks and many more things. They transported their owners by back, cart, and wagon in times before the car. They were an integral part of the Newfoundland way of life right up to the late 1940s and 50s and in some places beyond. In 1935 there were 9025 ponies in Newfoundland, and a healthy population existed up to the mid-70s and early 80s. Then the population plummeted. Perhaps the greatest causes of this decline were: machinery now took over the jobs once done by ponies, communities enacted no roaming laws limiting breeding and a food supply, owners were encouraged to have stallions gelded, thousands of the Newfoundland Ponies were sold to meat processing plants in Quebec from where the horse meat was sent to Belgium and France for human consumption.

In 1997, there were 144 known Newfoundland Ponies of which a sizeable number were geldings and aged mares. On September 12, 1997, the Government of Newfoundland declared the Newfoundland Pony as a Heritage Animal for the province. Restrictions have been made on the export and disposal of these animals, and the Newfoundland Pony Society named as the official public group responsible for registering, promoting and protecting this animal. Registered Newfoundland ponies now number about 250. An ongoing effort on the part of concerned individuals has stabilized the Newfoundland Pony population. However, the Newfoundland Pony continues to be classified as critically endangered.

Newfoundland Ponies are hardy, good-tempered, and sure-footed animals. Colors may include bay, black, brown, chestnut, dun, grey, roan and white (pink skin). They have a heavy coat which sometimes changes color and character seasonally. Height ranges between 11.0 and 14.2 hands and they work well for riding, driving, and light draft work, and can be ridden by both children and adults. *(cited from: http://afs.okstate.edu/breeds/horses/newfoundland/index.html)*

Paso Fino

Just as the Moorish conquest of Spain introduced a potentially promising breed to that country, so it was with Columbus' second voyage to the New World, when he transported the first horses to Santo Domingo - now the Dominican Republic. These animals were a mix of the Berber, the Jennet and the Andalusian. Future voyagers would add to their numbers in Mexico and South America, but the overall isolation established these as the ancestors to the Paso Fino. As remount stock for the conquistadors, the progeny of these horses were dispersed throughout the lands attacked by the invaders. Like pieces in a well-planned puzzle, the best of the contributing breeds became prominent in these isolated horses. Among other traits, their young enjoyed the hardiness of the Barb and the natural presence of the Andalusian. But most important and treasured was the incredibly even and smooth gait of the Jennet. Remarkably, that gait became the genetic stamp that identified this horse as the one we know today by the name Paso Fino.

It is the lateral four-beat gait that distinguishes the Paso Fino in the equestrian world. As it moves, the horse's feet fall in a natural lateral pattern instead of the more common diagonal pattern. Rather than trotting, the Paso Fino's medium speed is a corto, during which the rider is reassuringly seated. The basic gaits of the Paso Fino in order of speed are the paso fino, paso corto, and paso largo. They also walk and canter. These are not trained movements but are natural to the horse from the moment of its birth. Artificial training aids are not necessary to bring about this genetically inherent gait. A well-conditioned Paso Fino can travel at the corto for hours, and thanks to the smooth gait, so can the rider.

Elegant and with a brilliant style, the Paso Fino generally ranges in size from 13.2 hands to 15.2 hands. Colors run the spectrum with a variety of markings from chestnut, bay, palomino, black, grey and roan to pinto. It is a spirited yet gentle horse, intelligent and tractable. The Paso Fino has been bred for physical balance, with no exaggerated muscling or size in any portion of the horse.

Versatility is the passport to satisfied ownership for this popular equine. In addition to show and pleasure-trail abilities, the Paso Fino can be trained for a variety of uses. In competitive trail riding the endurance of the well-trained Paso Fino has earned the breed national honors. Its compact size and quickness have carved it a place on ranches where it becomes a hard-working partner and employee. In bird dog work, the Paso Fino not only demonstrates a fine temperament for field handling but is of a size that makes frequent mounting and dismounting easy. Because of its exceptionally smooth ride, it is the premier and prudent choice for those with back and neck injuries and arthritis, as well as for therapeutic riding programs for the handicapped. *(cited from: http://afs.okstate.edu/breeds/horses/pasofino/index.html)*

Peruvian Paso

The names, Paso Fino and Peruvian Paso, are deceptively similar. The two breeds stem from the same group of horses brought over to the Americas by the Spanish conquistadors who were typically mounted on Andalusians, Barbs and the now-extinct Jennet. This last breed of horse is perhaps the most important part of the Peruvian Paso/Paso Fino bloodline, as the Jennet was known for its unique four-beat ambling gait. As the Spanish spread across the South and North American continents, they brought their horses with them, breeding more stock from the original imported horses. The conquistador's horse was bred for stamina, beauty and most importantly the all-day-riding smooth gait.

History divides these 2 breeds: the horses who traveled west across South America to Peru stayed isolated in that coastal country, caught between the Pacific and the Andes. Among the Caribbean and Latin American countries, another variety of the conquistador horse remained, especially in Puerto Rico and Colombia. Both groups of horses retained their smooth gaits though they developed into vastly different expressions.

While each breed has its own names for the various speeds of the gait, the essence of the gait at all speeds and between both breeds is actually the same: a four-beat ambling lateral gait that is very smooth to ride. It's the way that the two breeds go about executing the gait that shows distinction between the Paso Fino and Peruvian Paso horse. The distinctions stem back to the theory of form to function. Developed for being a smooth-riding horse around the Spanish colonies of the Caribbean and Latin America, the Paso Fino gaits developed into smooth and quick-moving strides while maintaining the distinct four beats. Meanwhile, down in Peru, the Peruvian Paso was being bred specifically to cover long distances on mountain trails, creating a smooth-riding horse with a big, ground-covering stride *(cited from: http://www.horsenation.com/2015/01/27/ paso-fino-vs-peruvian-paso-whats-the-difference/)*

Rocky Mountain Horse (14,500 registered)

Tradition has it that around the turn of the century a young horse appeared in eastern Kentucky that gave rise to a line of horses that has been prized and treasured in this part of the country ever since. The basic characteristics are of a medium-sized horse of gentle temperament with an easy ambling four-beat gait. This gait made it the horse of choice on the farms and the rugged foothills of the Appalachians. It was a horse for all seasons. It could pull the plows in the small fields, work cattle, be ridden bareback by 4 children to the fishing hole, or to town comfortably on Saturday. They even performed well hitched to the buggy. Fancy barns and stalls were not necessary. Because of its cold-blooded nature, it tolerated the winters in Kentucky with a minimum of shelter. For these reasons, in small groups, the breed was preserved, sustained and gradually increased in the area. Naturally, out crossing with the local horses did occur but the basic characteristics of a strong genetic line have continued.

In Spout Springs, Kentucky, on the farm of Sam Tuttle, these horses found a nurturing ground. Sam, who had the concession for horseback riding at the Natural Bridge State Park, used these horses for many years to haul green and inexperienced people over rough and rugged trails. Old Tobe, his most treasured stallion, who fathered fine horses up until the ripe old age of 37, was as "sure" footed and as gentle a horse as could be found. He was the one that carried the young, the old, or the unsure over the mountain trails of Kentucky, without faltering, even though a breeding stallion. Everyone who rode the stallion fell in love with him. He had the perfect gait and temperament. Many of the present Rocky Mountain Horses carry his bloodline.

The breed is known for gentleness. It is an easy keeper and a wonderful riding horse with a strong heart and endurance. Today the Rocky Mountain Horse is being used as a pleasure horse, for trail, and competitive or endurance riding. As show horses, the breed is rapidly gaining in popularity because of its beauty and unique way of moving in the ring. The calm temperament of this horse makes it ideally suited for working around cattle and for 4-H projects. These horses have a lot of natural endurance, they are sure footed on rough ground and, because of their gait, they require a minimum of effort by both horse and rider so that together they can cover a greater distance with less tiring.

It is obvious that a haphazard and unorganized maintenance of this breed would eventually result in its dissipation and loss. For this reason, in the summer of 1986, those who were interested in the breed got together to form the Rocky Mountain Horse Association. The purpose of this association is to maintain the breed to increase the number of horses in the breed and expand knowledge of this fine horse. To that end, the association has established a registry which has shown steady and well-regulated growth in the number of horses registered. It is critical that standards be maintained, and a panel of examiners has been set up by the association to provide vigorous supervision to the growth and development of the breed. To achieve this ALL horses must be examined for breed characteristics and approved prior to breeding. The established characteristics for the breed are: (1) The horse must be of medium height from 14.2 to 16 hands, a wide chest sloping 45 degrees on the shoulder with bold eyes and well-shaped ears. (2) The horse must have a natural ambling four beat gait (single foot or rack), with no evidence of pacing. When the horse moves you can count four distinct hoof beats which produce a cadence of equal rhythm just like a walk, left hind, left fore, right hind, right fore. Each individual horse has its own speed and natural way of going, traveling at 7-20 miles per hour. This is a naturally occurring gait present from birth that does not require training aids or action devices. (3) It must be of good temperament and easy to manage. (4) All Rocky Mountain Horses have a solid body color. Facial markings are acceptable so long as they are not excessive. There may not be any white above the knee or hock. *(cited from: http://afs.okstate.edu/breeds/horses/rockymountain/index.html)*

Spanish Barb (147 Registered)

The Spanish-Barb traces its lineage through the Andalusian and Spanish Jennet horses brought to North America by the Spanish explorers during the 16th century. Both the Andalusian and the Jennet had evolved from the Barb horse of North Africa, which was brought to the Iberian Peninsula after the Moorish invasion of Spain in 711. In America, the Spanish-Barb was most prevalent in areas of Spanish settlement, in the Southeast and the Southwest. In the Southeast, the Spanish-Barb provided the foundation for both the Chickasaw and Choctaw Indian horses. Chickasaw blood would play a major role in the development of the American Quarter Horse. In the Southwest, they became the horse of the early Spanish and later Mexican cowboys and went on to form the basis for the wild Mustang herds of the West.

Over the years, the Spanish-Barb came close to being absorbed into the general horse population. The breed's survival today is due to the dedicated, but small-scale breeding carried on by a few individual families and ranchers. Unfortunately, few records were kept, and no attempt was made to register this rare and unique horse until the formation of the Spanish-Barb Breeders Association in 1972.

The Spanish-Barb weighs between 800 and 975 pounds and stands between 13.3 and 14.1 hands. They are noted for their smooth gait, comfortable ride, and surefootedness, which makes them an excellent horse for trail and endurance riding and ranch work. *(cited from: http://afs.okstate.edu/breeds/horses/spanishbarb/index.html)*

Standardbred

The origin of the Standardbred traces back to Messenger, an English Thoroughbred foaled in 1780 and exported to the United States in 1788. He was used to improve running horses in America but when a reform movement began putting pressure on the breeders of runners, trotting horse owners started breeding Messenger with their mares. For unknown reasons, Messenger never raced but his offspring became the fastest and best gaited trotters.

Messenger was the great-grandsire of Hambeltonian, *(left: Rysdyk's Hambletonian by Currier and Ives)* a famous trotter that became the foundation of the Standardbred breed. He was foaled in 1849 in New York. His dam was called the Charles Kent mare and was sired by a horse named Abdalla. Hambletonian was owned by a hired hand, William Ryskyk. His offspring dominated trotting races of the day. Messenger and Hambletonian were bred to Narraganset Pacers, Morgans and Thoroughbreds

The name "Standardbred" was first used in 1879, due to the fact that, in order to be registered, every Standardbred had to be able to trot a mile within the "standard" of 2 minutes and 30 seconds. Today, many Standardbreds race much faster than this original standard, with several pacing the mile within 1 minute, 50 seconds, and trotters only a few seconds slower than pacers. Slightly different bloodlines are found in trotters than pacers though both can trace their heritage back to Hambletonian. The stud book was formed in 1939, with the formation of the United States Trotting Horse Association.

Lou Dillon was the first Standardbred to trot the mile in less than 2 minutes. This talented, but temperamental mare performed this feat in Memphis, Tennessee, but was a west-coast horse, foaled in 1898 near Santa Ynez, California. High strung and hard to handle, she would only stay on her food when mixed with mashed carrots. She traveled extensively to as far away as Berlin, Moscow and Vienna to entertain spectators with her extraordinary abilities.

Dan Patch was the first Standardbred to pace the mile in less than 2 minutes. The race in Lexington, Kentucky was official (1:55 ¼ in 1905). The faster time of 1:55 was entered at the Minnesota State Fair in 1906 but was considered unofficial. This famous horse was foaled in Oxford, Indiana in 1896 and broke the speed record 14 times in the early 1900s. Dan Patch lost only two heats and never lost a race in his career. His record for the fastest pacing race stood for 54 years.

Standardbreds are able to perform the pace and all other horse gaits, including the canter. Standardbreds are best known for their level and sensible dispositions and are generally considered "easy keepers". Standardbred horses have refined, solid legs and powerful shoulders and hindquarters. Standardbreds have a wide range of height, from 14.1 to 17+ hands and most often are bay or the darker variation of bay called "brown," although other colors are not uncommon. Standardbreds are incredibly versatile. You will see them in dressage, jumping, eventing, western, endurance, parades, police work, search and rescue.

Tennessee Walker

The Civil War provided the opportunity for crossbreeding of the Confederate pacers with Union trotters thus creating the Planation Walking Horse. The horse gained popularity for the ease of its gaits and ability to stride with ease over hills and valleys in the rocky middle Tennessee terrain. Infused with the blood of Morgans, Standardbreds and Thoroughbreds, the Tennessee Walker came into being. The breed is seen in a variety of colors including brown, black, bay, chestnut, roan, palomino, white or gray. Their face, legs and body may also be marked with white. Tennessee walkers are 14.3 to 17 hands and weigh about 900 to 1,200 pounds. They have a long graceful neck, short back, well-built hindquarters, sloping shoulders, slender but strong legs, and sound feet. The Tennessee Walker's head is handsome and refined with bright eyes, prominent nostrils, and pointed well-shaped ears. Their manes and tails are usually left long and flowing.

Thoroughbred (1.3 million in the United States)

(left: Secretariat 1973 Triple Crown winner) Although the Thoroughbred is not a uniquely America breed, the early Thoroughbreds in America greatly influenced many of our American breeds. There are records of horse racing on Long Island as far back as 1665, the introduction of organized Thoroughbred racing to North America is traditionally credited to Governor Samuel Ogle of Maryland, through whose instigation racing "between pedigreed horses, in the English style" was first staged at Annapolis in 1745. As the country developed so did Thoroughbred racing, spreading across the nation from coast to coast until today the volume of racing in America far outweighs that of any other country in the world. American bloodlines, too, have come to be respected in the four corners of the earth

In early days, Thoroughbred breeding records were sparse and frequently incomplete, it being the custom, among other things, not to name a horse until it had proved outstanding ability. It was left to James Weatherby, through his own research and by consolidation of a number of privately kept pedigree records, to publish the first volume of the General Stud Book. He did this in 1791, listing the pedigrees of 387 mares, each of which could be traced back to Eclipse, a direct descendent of the Darley Arabian; Matchem, a grandson of the Godolphin Arabian; and Herod, whose great-great grandsire was the Byerly Turk. The General Stud Book is still published in England by Weatherby and Sons, Secretaries to the English Jockey Club.

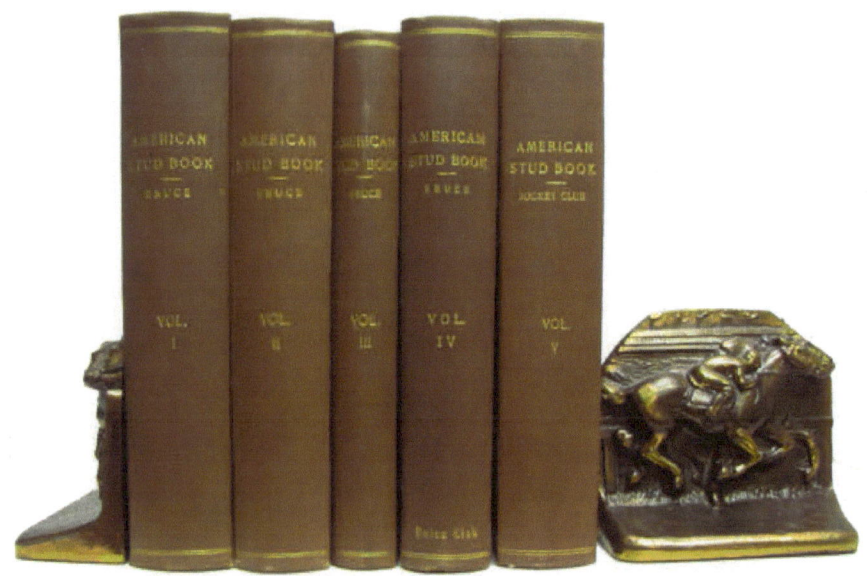

Several years later, as racing proliferated in the fast-expanding continent of North America, the need for a pedigree registry of American-bred Thoroughbreds, similar to the General Stud Book, became apparent. The first volume of The American Stud Book was published in 1873, by Col. Sanders D. Bruce, a Kentuckian who had spent almost a lifetime researching the pedigrees of American Thoroughbreds. Bruce closely followed the pattern of the first General Stud Book, producing 6 volumes of the register until 1896, when the project was taken over by The Jockey Club. Integrity of The American Stud Book is the foundation on which all Thoroughbred racing in North America depends. The Jockey Club manages one of the most sophisticated computer operations in the country. Its database holds the names of more than 1,800,000 horses on a master pedigree file, names which trace back to the late 1800s. The system also handles daily results of every Thoroughbred race in North America, as well as processing electronically transmitted pedigree and racing data from England, Ireland, France and other leading Thoroughbred racing countries around the world.

What began as a pastime and sporting amusement for the wealthy has now become a worldwide multi-million-dollar industry whose economic impact is widely felt at regional and national levels. From license fees and direct taxes on pari-mutuel handle Thoroughbred racing generates nearly $500,000,000 in government revenue each year. But this is relatively minor in comparison to the overall urban and rural economic contribution made by the wide and varied infrastructure of the racing and breeding industry as a whole. A recent estimate, for example, put the industry's contribution to the economy of New York State alone at more than $1.8 billion each year

The average height of today's Thoroughbred is a little over 16 hands, as opposed to the 14-hand average height of the horses from which the breed originated. The best guidelines for good conformation come from appreciation of what the body is required to do. Four slender legs must carry more than 1,000 pounds of body weight over extended distances, traveling at speeds of 35-40 miles per hour, yet still have the strength and suppleness to respond to changes of pace or direction as dictated by racing conditions.

But, although mechanical and engineering formula can be used to measure the most desirable dimensions and angles of the body's components, there is no way to measure the most important qualities of Thoroughbreds -- its courage, determination and will. *(cited from: http://afs.okstate.edu/breeds/horses/thoroughbred/index.html)*

Modern Breeds and Usage

The conformation of a horse will determine the horse's way of going. Each breed of horse has a very distinct conformation. A Morgan looks different from a Quarter Horse and will have a different way of going than a Quarter Horse. One way of going is not more correct than another. A horse with conformation not suitable for a show jumper could have excellent conformation for a cutting horse. That does not mean the cutting horse can't jump or the jumper can't cut cattle; it's just that a horse's form (conformation) and inherent ability lends itself to certain disciplines more than others. Some horses even excel at disciplines that they are not really cut out to do! The famous Olympic jumper, Nautical, was sired by a Quarter Horse. The well-known show jumper, Snowman, was considered a "plow horse" of mixed breed ancestry which for plow horses included inner breeding of Quarter Horse, Morgan and various draft horse types. So even though various conformation types and ways of going lend themselves to certain functions, there are exceptions to the rule – always evaluate horses with an open mind!

Remember, that in the early Americas, the gaits of the horse determined how the horse was used. Horses are no longer used strictly for utilitarian purposes. While gaits, conformation and way of going DO determine the *ideal* use for a horse, many breeds of horses participate, and even excel, in a variety of disciplines. REMEMBER - always evaluate horses with an open mind based on that horse's abilities, conformation and way of going.

Classification of Use by Gait in the Early Americas

Saddle
    Amblers
Agriculture
    Walking Horses
Harness
    Trotting Horses
Racing
    Amblers
    Trotting Horses
Ranching
    Herding Horses (walk, trot, canter, fast sprint, agile)

Classification of Modern Use by Abilities

Each horse type has a predisposition towards specific disciplines. Below is a list of various horse disciplines and the abilities needed for that discipline.
- Abilities are listed from most important to least important for each discipline.
- To help determine what discipline a horse is best suited for, look at what abilities seem to be highest for that horse.
- Conformation and way of going also play important roles in determining a suitable discipline for a horse.

DISCIPLINE	ABILITIES
Barrel Racing	Agility, Speed, Strength, Balance
Cross Country	Stamina, Strength, Agility, Balance
Cutting	Agility, Intelligence, Strength, Speed
Dressage	Movement, Balance, Tempo, Strength
Driven Dressage	Movement, Balance, Strength, Tempo
Endurance	Stamina, Speed, Agility, Tempo
Harness Racing	Speed, Stamina, Strength, Tempo
Hunter	Movement, Strength, Tempo, Balance
In-Hand Jumping	Intelligence, Agility, Strength, Stamina
Log Pull	Strength, Stamina, Movement, Tempo
Marathon Driving	Strength, Stamina, Tempo, Intelligence

Obstacle Driving	Strength, Agility, Stamina, Balance
Pole Bending	Speed, Agility, Intelligence, Balance
Racing	Speed, Stamina, Strength
Reining	Agility, Strength, Movement, Balance
Saddleseat	Balance, Agility, Movement, Intelligence
Show Jumping	Balance, Strength, Agility, Speed
Sprint Racing	Speed, Strength, Agility
Steeplechasing	Speed, Agility, Strength, Stamina
Western Pleasure	Intelligence, Balance, Movement, Tempo
Western Trail	Agility, Balance, Intelligence, Stamina
Working Ranch	Intelligence, Agility, Balance, Strength

(cited from: http://www.horseworldonline.net/forum/viewtopic.php?t=1235)

CONCLUSION

Today, there are many breeds of horses in the Americas that are the result of cross breeding the early breeds as well as cross breeding many breeds and types of horses from all around the world.

It's difficult to determine how many horses there are of each breed in the Americas; a portion of the population— probably a significant one—was never registered, or its registrations have gotten lost with changes of ownership. Membership and registration fees are expensive, and the majority of Americans are involved in horse activities that don't require registry/association affiliation, thus papers are not a compelling need throughout the horse-owning population. Of the hundred or so U.S. registries, most record bloodlines to maintain a "pure" genetic pool by requiring that newly registered animals be the offspring of two parents who are already in the studbook. Today DNA testing is required by the more rigorous organizations to assure authenticity of parentage. Other studbooks are "open," meaning that occasional outcrossing is allowed with a few other specified breeds. The quarter horse studbook, for instance, has permitted breeding with Thoroughbreds, among others, particularly in producing racing stock. In addition to or in lieu of recording by bloodline, breeds are now defined by other parameters. Almost a quarter of the registries listed in the AHC (American Horse Council) directory accept horses on the basis of physical appearance.

A study commissioned by the American Horse Council Foundation and conducted by the Barents Group concluded that there are currently 9.2 million horses in the United States alone! *(cited from: Demographics of US Horse Population; http://www.humanesociety.org/assets/pdfs/hsp/soaiv_07_ch10.pdf)*

The Americas are a melting pot of peoples AND horses! Horses have indeed played an important role in the development of the Americas – but that is another story….

SOURCES

Books, Research Papers

Boniface, Katrin. *Horse Power: Social Evolution in Medieval Europe*. Thesis for Master of Arts in History in the College of Social Sciences California State University, Fresno, May 2015

De Steiguer, J. Edward. *Wild Horses of the West: History and Politics of American Mustangs*. Tucson. University of Arizona Press, 2011

Edwards, Elwyn Hartley. *Encyclopedia of the Horse*. Quarry Bay, Hong Kong: Mandarin Publishers Limited, 1977

Edwards, Peter. *Horse and Man in Early Modern England*. London, Hambledon Continuum, 2007

Gruenberg, Bonnie U. *The Wild Horse Dilemma: Conflicts and Controversies of the Atlantic Coast Herds*. Starsburg, Pennsylvania, Quagga Press, 2015

Kirsan, Kathleen Hiney. *North American Sport Horse Breeder*. Indianapolis, Indiana, Dog Ear Publishing, 2013

Muybridge, Eadweard. *Descriptive Zoopraxograph,* 1893

Lynghauh, Fran. The Official Horse Breeds Standards Guide: The Complete Guide to the Standards of All North American Equine Breed Associations. Minneapolis, Minnesota, Voyageur Press, 2009

Wallace, John Hankins, *The Horse of America in His Derivation, History and Development*. New York, Published by the Author, 1897

Oklahoma State University's Division of Agricultural Sciences and Natural Resources was a valuable source for breed descriptions.

Internet Sources
http://www.horseworldonline.net/forum/viewtopic.php?t=1235
http://articles.mcall.com/1988-03-06/entertainment/2614046_1_five-horses-conestoga-breed
http://en.chateauversailles.fr/discover/history/horses-versailles#the-king's-horses
http://horsechannel.com/horse-breeds/profiles/barb-horse-horse-breed.aspx
http://horseoftheamericas.com/conformation.html
http://josfamilyhistory.com/stories/hooker.htm
http://marielynnhammond.com/LegacyCanadians/1098845.htm
http://marielynnhammond.com/LegacyCanadians/1098845.htm
http://mayflowerhistory.com/livestock/
http://moorishharem.com/the-moorish-hunting-trio-the-barb-horse-the-noble-sighthound-and-the-falcon/
http://northcarolinahistory.org/encyclopedia/lucas-vasques-de-ayllon-1475-1526/
http://padrekino.com/kino-legacy/horseman/
http://padrekino.com/kino-legacy/horseman/
http://ruralfloridaliving.blogspot.com/2012/04/ponce-de-leon-and-florida-livestock.html
http://virginiahistoryseries.org/linked/unit%2011.%20early%20history%20of%20horses%20in%20virginia.all%20slides.pdf
http://welcome.topuertorico.org/history.shtml
 http://www.almc.army.mil/alog/issues/sepoct99/ms409.htm
http://www.ansi.okstate.edu/breeds
http://www.biografiadechile.cl/detalle.php?IdContenido=373&IdCategoria=8&IdArea=35&TituloPagina=Historia%20de%20Chile
http://www.boweryboyshistory.com/2011/05/why-go-to-kentucky-new-yorks.html

http://www.chincoteague.com/ponies.html
http://www.esdaw.eu/horse---breeding.html
http://www.galiceno.org/index.html
http://www.galiceno.org/index.html
http://www.history.org/Almanack/life/trades/traderural_horses.cfm
http://www.history.org/foundation/journal/winter08/horses.cfm
http://www.horsenation.com/2015/01/27/paso-fino-vs-peruvian-paso-whats-the-difference/
http://www.horsenation.com/2016/10/04/warhorses-the-dawn-horse/
http://www.humanesociety.org/assets/pdfs/hsp/soaiv_07_ch10.pdf
http://www.iboston.org/mcp.php?pid=taleOfTwoBostons
http://www.imh.org/exhibits/online/legacy-of-the-horse/colonial-horses/
http://www.imh.org/exhibits/online/legacy-of-the-horse/colonial-horses/
http://www.lrgaf.org/articles/spanish-horse-progeny.htm
http://www.manythings.org/voa/history/4.html
http://www.medievalists.net/2015/12/horse-power-social-evolution-in-medieval-europe/
http://www.mexconnect.com/articles/682-the-aztecs-speak-an-aztec-account-of-the-conquest-of-mexico
http://www.museumofthehorse.org/a-look-at-the-turkoman-horse-in-iran/
http://www.namarchador.org/breed/
 http://www.newenglandhistoricalsociety.com/narragansett-pacer-lost-horse-new-england-colonies/
http://www.oldstonehousefarm.com/PDFs/conquistadorsill.pdf
http://www.pbs.org/gunsgermssteel/variables/horses.html
http://www.providencejournal.com/opinion/commentary/20140207-robert-a.-geake when-wolves-ranged-new-england.ece
http://www.quahog.org/factsfolklore/index.php?id=210
http://www.ranchodelsueno.com/blog.html
http://www.ranchodelsueno.com/blog.html
http://www.sciencemag.org/news/2017/06/most-modern-horses-came-just-two-ancient-lineages
http://www.scottsdaleshow.com/club-info/breed-information
http://www.sport-horse-breeder.com/american-breed-development.html
http://www.sport-horse-breeder.com/irish-hobby.html
http://www.standardbredfanclub.com/history.html

http://www.thecanadianencyclopedia.ca/en/article/horse/
http://www.theequinest.com/breeds/baguales/
http://www.theequinest.com/breeds/banker-pony/
http://www.walkerswest.com/History/MysteriousNarragansettPacer.htm
http://www3.sympatico.ca/goweezer/canada/z00cartier4.htm
https://anthrosource.onlinelibrary.wiley.com/doi/pdf/10.1525/aa.1940.42.1.02a00060
https://anthrosource.onlinelibrary.wiley.com/doi/pdf/10.1525/aa.1939.41.1.02a00100
https://archive.org/stream/horseraisinginco00phil/horseraisinginco00phil_djvu.txt
https://archive.org/stream/horseraisinginco00phil/horseraisinginco00phil_djvu.txt p921
https://archive.org/stream/horseraisinginco00phil/horseraisinginco00phil_djvu.txt
https://awionline.org/content/wild-horses-native-north-american-wildlife
https://blogs.scientificamerican.com/tetrapod-zoology/spots-stripes-and-spreading-hooves-in-the-horses-of-the-ice-age/
https://books.google.com/books?id=A-n63276g-AC&pg=PT98&lpg=PT98&dq#v=onepage&q&f=false
https://dermotmccabe.com/2015/10/21/the-irish-hobby-horse/
https://en.wikipedia.org/wiki/Carolina_Marsh_Tacky
https://en.wikipedia.org/wiki/Palfrey
https://historicjamestowne.org/selected-artifacts/horse-bones-2/
https://livestockconservancy.org/index.php/heritage/internal/americancream
https://livestockconservancy.org/index.php/heritage/internal/colonialspanish
https://sites.google.com/site/atimelineofamerica/1611
https://thetyee.ca/News/2013/03/06/Horse-Dung-Big-Shift/
https://tkmorin.wordpress.com/tag/baron-de-lery-et-de-st-just/
https://www.americancowboy.com/ranch-life-archive/history-vaquero
https://www.americanheritage.com/content/fox-hunting-america
https://www.americanheritage.com/content/how-indian-got-horse
https://www.britannica.com/animal/horse/Evolution-of-the-horse#ref239134
https://www.britannica.com/biography/Panfilo-de-Narvaez
https://www.britannica.com/sports/horse-racing
https://www.britishbattles.com/war-of-the-revolution-1775-to-1783/
https://www.elkrivergr.com/blog/the-history-of-posting-the-trot-myths-debunked

https://www.equisearch.com/articles/spanish-horse-breeds
https://www.equisearch.com/articles/spanish-horse-breeds
https://www.euskalkazeta.com/basques-in-the-americas-1492-to-1592/
https://www.hiddentrails.com/article/horses_gaits.aspx
https://www.horsetalk.co.nz/2014/10/07/north-americas-wild-horses-native/
https://www.horsetalk.co.nz/2014/10/07/north-americas-wild-horses-native/
https://www.livescience.com/27686-mustangs.html
https://www.livescience.com/9589-surprising-history-america-wild-horses.html
https://www.livescience.com/9589-surprising-history-america-wild-horses.html
https://www.mnn.com/earth-matters/animals/stories/mustangs-of-the-west-why-this-american-icon-is-disappearing
https://www.nationalgeographic.org/encyclopedia/ranching/
https://www.ncpedia.org/biography/ayll%C3%B3n-lucas-v%C3%A1squez-de
https://www.reddit.com/r/AskHistorians/comments/3eu40z/were_there_horses_in_the_americas_before_columbus/
https://www.smithsonianmag.com/history/off-to-the-races-2266179
www.criollo-horse.com/en/history-of-the-criollo-breed.html

www.ingramcontent.com/pod-product-compliance
Lightning Source LLC
Chambersburg PA
CBHW040630100526

44584CB00035B/287